FAMILIAR

BIRDS

of the
NORTHWEST

**Covering birds
commonly found in
Oregon, Washington, Idaho
Northern California and Western Canada**

Harry B. Nehls

with paintings by
**R. Bruce Horsfall, Amy C. Fisher
L. B. McQueen and Zella M. Schultz**

illustrations by
Joe E. Evanich

Printed in U.S.A.

PORTLAND AUDUBON SOCIETY
5151 N.W. Cornell Road
Portland, Oregon 97210

ACKNOWLEDGMENTS

"Familiar Birds of the Northwest" incorporates much of what is found in "Familiar Birds of Northwest Forests, Fields and Gardens" by David B. Marshall, and "Familiar Birds of Northwest Shores and Waters" by Harry B. Nehls. Special recognition must again be given to all who made those publications possible as their efforts contributed much also to this book.

Kenneth C. Batchelder has been primarily responsible for the singular success of the entire "Familiar Birds" series. He promoted and guided each book through to production and provided the business acumen needed. Without his efforts it is doubtful that any of these books would have appeared.

John B. Crowell, Jr. and James G. Olson edited and reviewed the manuscripts for this publication. The text reflects many of their suggestions.

Many members of the Audubon Society of Portland have actively worked on making the entire "Familiar Birds" series a success. Without continued support of all the Society's members this publication would not have been possible.

First Printing August 1981   15,000 copies
Second Printing October 1983   10,000 copies

Printing by:
Dynagraphics, Inc.
300 N.W. 14th Avenue
Portland, Oregon 97209

Color separations by:
Wy'east Color, Inc.
4321 S.W. Corbett Ave.
Portland, Oregon 97201

© 1981 Audubon Society of Portland
Library of Congress Card Number 81-66453
I S B N Number 0-931686-05-9

INTRODUCTION

"Familiar Birds of the Northwest" combines, revises and enlarges two successful publications of the Portland Audubon Society: "Familiar Birds of Northwest Forests, Fields and Gardens" by David B. Marshall and "Familiar Birds of Northwest Shores and Waters" by Harry B. Nehls. Much of the material from the two earlier publications has been incorporated into this new book to which 80 illustrations and species accounts were added to encompass the enlarged geographic area brought within the scope of this publication. The area now covered includes all of Oregon, Washington, Idaho, Northern California and most of the birds of Western Canada.

This publication is prepared as an easy-to-use guide to the common birds found in the Pacific Northwest. The account of each species includes a brief description of points useful in identifying the bird in the field. Rare or uncommon birds, but with distinctly different color patterns or field points, are also discussed, but not illustrated.

Further information on nesting, habitat, and habits of Northwestern birds can be obtained by consulting larger and more complete field guides and from other ornithological literature, a few of the most pertinent of which are listed in the reference section.

The illustrations in this book depict birds in one or more of the plumages in which they are usually found in our region. In addition to usually slight plumage variations between males and females of some species, breeding plumage may differ markedly from winter dress in many species; juvenile plumage differences also add to the variations. Consequently, not all plumages of many of the species illustrated can be shown. In designating plumage differences in picture captions, the standard symbols are used: male ♂; female ♀.

Many birds can be identified readily in any plumage while others can be quite difficult. It is recommended, therefore, that an observer learn to recognize birds by reference to size, shape, song, particular habits, or by some other characteristic in addition to plumage colorations.

In the descriptive accounts, some comment is usually made on distribution and seasonal occurrences. Although individuals of a given species may be found almost anywhere, each species is partial to a particular habitat or series of habitats and except in migration will seldom stray from it. Reference is made in this book to the habitat requirements for most of the species described.

Nomenclature utilized follows the 1983 edition of the American Ornithologists' Union's "Checklist of North American Birds." The latest revision conforms to the North American Checklist and to the International Checklist. Arrangements of species in the checklist are based on a classification system in which related birds are grouped together, with the most primitive forms listed first. This standard classification begins with the loons and ends with the most highly specialized land birds.

Measurement of total length, and in the case of larger birds, the wingspan, are shown in inches with the illustrations under the designation "L" and "W." These dimensions were freely copied from Robbins, Bruun and Zim, "A Guide to Field Identification Birds of North America" (Golden Press, New York 1966), who based their measurements on live males using tip-of-bill to tip-of-tail for the length measurement.

BIRD CLASSIFICATION

Birds, like other animals, are grouped first into large categories called orders, and then into families of which there are generally more than one to an order. Some families are divided into subfamilies. Families or subfamilies, whichever the case may be, are in turn broken down into genera, and the genera into species. The scientific name of a bird (or other animal or plant) consists of the genus (singular of genera) name followed by the species name. It may also include a third name which designates a subspecies, also called a race. Except where there are distinct field characters, this book does not treat subspecies. Most cannot be identified except by specialists using museum specimens.

Serious bird students learn family characteristics for they help locate and identify birds from a field manual.

Order and family groupings for the birds listed in this book follow, with common and scientific names and page references to the text for each species.

Order CICONIIFORMES
Family ARDEIDAE Herons and Bitterns

Family THRESKIORNITHIDAE Ibis

Order ANSERIFORMES
Family ANATIDAE Swans, Geese, and Ducks

Order APODIFORMES

Order CORACIIFORMES

Order PICIFORMES

Order PASSERIFORMES

xii

The size and shape of a bird's bill is an important field point in identifying in what group it can be found. Hawks and owls have heavy hooked bills for tearing flesh while sparrows and finches break open seeds with short, thick, pointed bills. Birds that gather their food from foliage and crannies have thin pointed bills. The swallows, swifts, and nighthawks have very large mouths with weak broad bills for gathering flying insects. Ducks have soft broad bills with sieves to filter food from mud and water. Many shorebirds have long, thin, soft bills with feeling senses near the tips in order to search out animal life in mud and sand.

A number of birds have rather long, medium, all-purpose bills. Some are long and sharp for spearing or grasping fish. Herons, egrets, loons and several other water birds have this type, while woodpeckers have similar bills that are much stronger for chiseling wood. Robins, crows, blackbirds and starlings have similar but weaker bills for gathering fruit, soft grains and insects.

The tremendous bill of the pelican has a large pouch to aid in catching fish. Cormorants have similar pouches but they are much smaller and not much help in catching food. Crossbills have specially designed bills for prying seeds out of cones. In order to pick up loose seeds from the ground crossbills must use their tongue as their bill cannot grasp loose objects. Other birds also utilize their tongues in conjuction with their bills in order to obtain food. Hummingbirds have long tube-like tongues and long thin bills for sucking up nectar and insects from flowers.Certain sea birds have tubular nostrils that filter salt from the air and water they ingest.

illustrations by J. E. Evanich

short heavy seed eating bills
sparrows and finches

medium all-purpose bills
jays, robins and blackbirds

weak, wide bills for gathering
flying insects.
nighthawk, swallows, flycatcher

thin pointed bills for
gleaning insects.
warblers, wrens

soft broad bills for sifting
mud and grazing.
ducks, geese

heavy hooked bills for
tearing flesh.
hawks, owls, shrike

long, thin, soft bills for
probing mud and sand.
shorebirds

long, heavy, pointed bills
for grasping and spearing.
herons, loons, grebes

In most birds the foot has four toes, a hind toe and three front toes. In each group of birds their feet have been modified to fit the needs of that particular group. Swimming birds have developed webs between the toes; predatory birds have sharp strong talons; wading birds have long legs to keep their bodies well above the water and long toes for support.

Perching birds make up the largest group of birds. Their tough, thin toes can tightly grasp a tree branch or power line so firmly that it takes great power to pry them loose. A special muscle in the toes tightens automatically when the bird bends its legs so that it can sleep or rest without losing its hold on the perch. Birds of prey have similar toes but they are modified even more into powerful talons so that they can grasp and kill their prey. These talons can also be folded into a 'fist,' allowing the bird to strike down a large bird or mammal without actually grasping it. In woodpeckers, and a few other species, the foot has two toes facing forward and two behind. This gives added support as the bird travels up and down tree trunks and other vertical surfaces. In many ground loving birds the feet and toes are fully feathered to give added warmth and as an aid in traveling over snow and soft ground. Others have very strong toes for scratching and digging.

Birds that live and feed about water have specially modified toes for their particular needs. Pelicans and cormorants have huge leathery webs connecting all four toes for extra power in maneuvering their huge bodies. Most other swimming and diving birds have webs only between the three front toes. Some water birds have such huge webbed feet that they use them as rudders in flight. Loons, grebes, coots and phalarope do not have webs but flaps, or lobes, edging each toe. There spread out broadly when pushed against the water, but fold tightly against the toes as the leg is brought forward. Some birds have partial webs at the base of the toes for support on soft sand or mud. These birds are said to be semipalmated.

All birds use their feet for scratching and grooming their plumage. In some species a toe or nail is especially modified with a small comb for better grooming of their feathers.

*grasping feet for
perching birds.
finches, warblers*

*two toes forward and two
back for vertical support.
woodpeckers*

webbed toes for swimming and for support on soft mud.
ducks, geese

strong legs and feet with claws for scratching.
grouse, quail

strong, sharp talons for grasping and holding.
hawks and owls

long legs and toes for wading.
herons, shorebirds

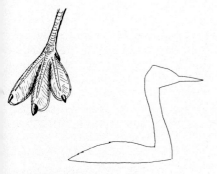

lobed feet for swimming and support and ease in movement.
grebes, coot

huge fully webbed feet including hind toe.
pelicans, cormorants

TIPS FOR BIRDING

Train yourself to identify birds through observing the following: overall size; shape of body, head, tail and wings; type of bill; length and color of legs; foot structure; posture; locomotion, such as hopping or walking and straight, undulating, flapping or soaring flight; field marks like eye stripes and wing bars; flocking habits.

Observations from a blind or from the window of a parked car will allow good close studies not possible in other ways. Binoculars and spotting scopes are an aid in bird identification. The 7x35 size is most popular for general use in binoculars, 20 power for scopes.

Observations of the color and pattern of the plumages is the easiest but not always the best way to identify a bird. Familiarize yourself with birds' habits while they are feeding or resting and in which habitat type they prefer. In spring and summer go afield in early morning to take advantage of the birds' greatest activity period.

Migration periods are the most productive. The peak of the spring migration is from mid-April to late May. The fall migration is more leisurely and the peak extends throughout August and September.

Go afield alone or with a few companions. Groups are good for instruction purposes only.

Train yourself to see what you are looking at and listen to what you hear. It is surprising how much we miss unless we take the time to learn this basic rule.

Most waterbirds are wary and occur in large open areas where a close approach is seldom allowed unless the observer is accepted. Birds can often be approached closely by casually walking toward them with the sun fully lighting the observer. A stealthy approach is seldom successful. Waterbirds become quite flighty in windy weather, and are hard to approach. Early morning is often calmer than later in the day and the birds are often more easily approached at that time.

In tidal areas most waterbirds feed in periods of low water and rest at high tide. Learning the feeding and resting areas will greatly increase the chance of a successful day afield.

Keep a field diary. Make it detailed.

Join your local Audubon Society. Experienced birders provide guidance on places to go, conduct field trips, and aid in identification. It is enjoyable to share your findings. Membership brings, in addition, the opportunity to join in many activities, including such matters as conservation, lectures, and usually a club publication with information on current birding of interest. Most Audubon Societies are branches of the National Audubon Society, bringing additional information on national problems and activities.

ABOUT THE ARTISTS: R. Bruce Horsfall, born in Clinton, Iowa, in 1868, studied art in Cincinnati, Munich, and Paris, specializing in portraiture and landscapes. He subsequently became a naturalist and took up natural history painting. Mr. Horsfall was active with the Oregon (now Portland) Audubon Society in the 1920's when his skill as a bird painter was nationally recognized. He then joined the staff of the old *Nature Magazine* as a full-time artist and painted museum backdrops for the American Museum of Natural History in New York. He died in 1948.

Zella M. Schultz, a native of Washington State, studed both art and biology at Western Washington College and for her M.S. degree, awarded by the University of Wasington, did a thesis on plumage characteristics of gulls. She was a combination ornithologist-artist known for both her bird paintings and specialized knowledge of gulls. She taught courses in bird identification for the University of Washington School of Forestry and the Seattle Audubon Society. She died in 1974.

L. B. McQueen is a native of Pennsylvania. His interest in birds began in childhood. He studied biology at Idaho State College in the early 60's and worked for the Idaho State Game Commission on predatory relationships of Golden Eagles and Antelope. He came to Oregon in 1963, and studied art at the University of Oregon. He has been employed as a graphic designer, free-lanced in painting and illustrating, and taught classes in painting, drawing, and in ornithology. Presently, he is working on illustrations for South American bird guides. His paintings continue on national exhibition. An exhibit at the Smithsonian Institution, Washington, D.C., in the fall of 1981 included many of his works.

Amy C. Fisher, while at the Department of Biological Sciences at the University of Idaho in Moscow, was commissioned to paint many of the bird illustrations for this publication. Her illustrations appear in many publications, including *Mammals of the Northwest,* published by the Seattle Audubon Society.

Joe E. Evanich, born in San Jose, Ca., has lived in many sections of the Pacific Northwest. He is currently enrolled in Eastern Oregon State College in La Grande, Or. where he is studying land-use planning. His illustrations appear in many Oregon publications, most regularly in the Oregon Field Ornithologists' publication *Oregon Birds,* and the Audubon Society of Portland's newsletter *The Audubon Warbler.*

ABOUT THE AUTHOR: Harry B. Nehls is a native of Iowa. He came to Portland, Oregon while still quite young. He had a natural interest in birds that developed into a life-long hobby. Since 1957, he has been employed by the United States Postal Service at the Main Portland Post Office. Mr. Nehls is a Past President of the Portland Audubon Society, and is Field Notes Editor of the Society's monthly newsletter, the *Audubon Warbler*. He is a member of the American Ornithologists' Union, State Coorinator for the U.S. Fish and Wildlife Service's Breeding Bird Surveys, and former co-editor with John B. Crowell, Jr. for the North Pacific Coast Region of *American Birds*.

Z. M. Schultz

Common Loon   Summer   Winter   L 24″ W 58″

The heavy-bodied **LOONS** are so adapted to a water environment that they are almost helpless on land. The large paddle-like feet, so marvelous in propelling the birds under water, are set so far back on the body that they are of little use for walking or standing. A loon can propel itself on land only by pushing along on its breast. Small fish constitute most of their diet, which they catch by diving and swimming under water. They use both wings and feet for propulsion, and can dive to depths of 200 feet. During the nesting season, loons are found in the far north, or on forest lakes and ponds. In these places their weird calls are a part of the wild.

Loons migrate to the sea coast to spend the winter months on protected bays, estuaries, and larger rivers. In migration large numbers can be seen flying just off the ocean beaches. Loons do not fly in formation like many other water birds but scatter over a large area, each bird going its own way. In winter the three species of loons regularly seen on the coast have similar plumages, dark gray above and white below. The loons are birds of great curiosity. They can be lured by unusual movements like the fluttering of a handkerchief.

The **COMMON LOON** is the species most often seen, especially in winter, along the coast. It is also noted at this season on inland fresh-water lakes and rivers. The heavy head, neck, dagger-like bill, and bulky body are distinctive. Common Loons assume their black and white breeding plumage early and retain it late enough in the year so that birds in this dress are frequently seen on the wintering grounds.

Arctic Loon   Winter   Summer   L 18" W 47"

The **ARCTIC LOON** appears as a smaller edition of the Common Loon. A close look will identify a bird of this species by its smaller size, less massive bill, and more sloping forehead. In summer Arctic Loons have a distinctive plumage. The gray head contrasts with the black back, which has two rows of white bars. The white throat is streaked at the sides with black and has a glossy, black patch. Arctic Loons sometimes occur in fairly large groups, riding out stormy weather in the lee of some protected headland or in the sheltered corner of an estuary.

The **RED-THROATED LOON** in summer dress is a handsome bird of black and white, with streaked hind neck, and bright chestnut throat. In winter the back is grayer than those of other loons; the bird's best field mark at this season is the bill, the lower mandible of which is sloped upward. Seldom do more than a few Red-throated Loons gather together, even on the salt-water bays and estuaries which they frequent in winter.

Red-Throated Loon   Summer   Winter   L 17" W 44"

Red-Necked Grebe   Summer   Winter   L 13″ W 32″

Z. M. Schultz

Like loons, **GREBES** are highly aquatic. They share with the loons an almost complete helplessness on land and a high degree of swimming and diving ability. Grebes tend to be short-bodied, long-necked birds, while loons are long-bodied and short-necked. Small fish, insects, shrimp, water plants, and other small life found in the water are standard diet items for grebes. They nest in fresh-water marshes where floating nest platforms are constructed from marsh vegetation.

Most species of grebes migrate to salt water to winter, but they do not entirely lose their affinity for marshes. At this season individual grebes can be found in well-protected inland marshes or ponds. The feet are peculiar. In place of having webs connecting the toes, as in other swimming birds, each toe is individually webbed or lobed. Grebes share this odd footwear with coots and phalaropes. A grebe can dive in a flash or slowly drop out of sight. It sometimes plays submarine with just its head and neck out of water.

The **RED-NECKED GREBE,** named for its most prominent summer plumage feature, occurs along the Pacific Coast only in winter or in migration; it is at no time common. A few can be found each winter in coastal bays and estuaries. Occasionally, large winter-time flocks are encountered in Puget Sound and about Vancouver Island. Red-necked Grebes can best be identified in winter by the rather thick, yellowish bill, and by the whitish crescent—sometimes suffused—on the side of the gray head.

Seldom noted in summer, the **HORNED GREBE** becomes common in the Pacific Northwest during the winter on protected salt-water bays and estuaries. At this time they appear to be small, gray and white, duck-like birds, usually occurring singly or in small scattered groups. Seldom are grebes seen flying. Instead, they normally escape by diving and swimming.

Horned Grebe   Summer   Winter   L 9½″ W 24″

3

Z. M. Schultz

The **EARED GREBE** is uncommon west of the Cascades. It is a common nesting bird in the marshes of the Great Basin. A few appear outside the breeding season in coastal or inland localities west of the Cascade Mountains. Eared Grebes in winter can be distinguished from Horned Grebes by the much grayer neck and slimmer, slightly upturned bill.

The distinctive and perky **WESTERN GREBE** is the largest of the grebes. The swan-like neck and yellow, stiletto bill are distinctive. Black above and white below, the "swan grebe" was almost wiped out by the millinery trade at the turn of the century, when its gleaming white breast feathers were in great demand. The Western Grebe is famed for its bizarre courtship dance. This species is relatively abundant in the marshes of the Great Basin where it breeds. The Western Grebe keeps its black and white plumage the year around. Outside the breeding season, large flocks are sometimes seen gathered well out in bays or off the beaches on the open ocean.

The **PIED-BILLED GREBE** is distinguished from other grebes by its brownish plumage. Although there is some migratory movement to coastal locations, this species does not favor salt water in winter, but prefers small fresh-water ponds and marshes the year around. Pied-billed Grebes are normally found singly, or in very small groups, and seldom far from the heavy cover they favor. These grebes eat a variety of aquatic animals and are not restricted to fish; thus these small divers are often found on bodies of water containing few or no fish.

Like some of the grebes, the **AMERICAN COOT** nests in fresh-water marshes and moves to open water in winter. Underwater plants, algae, and grasses form the bulk of its food. Small animal life and seeds will also be taken when available. Coots can dive fairly well, but they are more often seen tipping like a duck or grazing on shore. They are often found among the wintering flocks of ducks about our city parks and golf courses but are seldom far from the protection of some nearby water to which they quickly run when approached. Their dark, round bodies, whitish chicken-like bills, and big lobed feet identify these birds. Many of the weird and unusual bird noises heard in the marshes and about water-bird gathering places can be attributed to these avian clowns. Their love of shallow, marshy edges gives this species the nickname "mud hen." Not a true duck or grebe, the coot is a member of the marsh-loving rail family.

Eared Grebe   Winter   Summer

Z. M. Schultz
L 9″ W 23″

Western Grebe

Z. M. Schultz
L 18″ W 40″

Pied-billed Grebe L 9″   American Coots L 12″ W 25″

Z. M. Schultz

A number of species of birds are truly pelagic or ocean oriented. Although they occur a few miles offshore, they are seldom seen from land. Among these are the albatrosses, storm-petrels, the majority of shearwaters, and the fulmar. The most abundant and readily seen of the pelagics are the **SHEARWATERS.** Skimming just over the waves on set wings, these gull-like seabirds execute one of the most marvelous migrations in the animal kingdom. Reared in burrows dug on islands off New Zealand, Australia, and the southern tip of South America during our winter, these tube-nosed birds gather in tremendous flocks in March to migrate north. Passing offshore in May and June, these birds travel to the Aleutians before returning. The southward flight closely follows the ocean beaches. During August and September shearwaters sometimes enter the larger bays and river mouths. At times these birds can be seen in flocks of many thousands, passing in endless procession for long periods of time. Small fish and squid form most of their diet. The birds gorge so heavily at times that they fly with difficulty.

Several species of shearwater occur offshore. The most common is the **SOOTY SHEARWATER.** Dark with a flash of white in the under wings, these birds constitute most of the great flocks. If, on occasion, the observer distinguishes an infrequent white-bellied bird, it is probably the less common **PINK-FOOTED SHEARWATER** (not illustrated).

Close relatives of the shearwaters breed in the Northern Hemisphere. Among these, the **NORTHERN FULMAR** is most often seen from the northern Pacific Coast. Breeding on cliffs edging the Bering Sea and on islands in the Aleutians, these birds fly southward in fall to winter well off the Pacific Coast of North America. Large numbers sometimes occur just off the beaches as the birds migrate. Fulmars can be identified by the "barrelroll" effect as they skim the water, then rise high in the air before returning to the surface. Although most common early in the fall, the species may appear at any time during the winter months. Numbers are at rare intervals washed up dead on the beaches, as fierce winter storms, shortages of food, or possibly some epidemic overtakes them. Fulmars appear as stubby, gull-like birds with long, narrow wings. Two plumages occur, one gray and white, like a gull, and another smoky gray throughout. Fulmars have heavy yellow bills with prominent nostril tubes.

The dainty, little, pearl-gray **FORK-TAILED STORM-PETREL** and the almost black **LEACH'S STORM-PETREL** (Petrels not illustrated) are uncommon breeding birds on the rocks off the entire West Coast. These birds are seldom seen, as they are for the most part nocturnal near shore. They are more often found many miles from land and are seen fluttering about fishing boats searching for scraps. Petrels are similar to shearwaters and share with them many habits, including nesting in burrows.

Sooty Shearwater

Z. M. Schultz

L 16″ W 43″

Northern Fulmar   Dark Phase   Light Phase   L 18″ W 42″

Z. M. Schultz

Brown Pelican   Summer

L. B. McQueen
L 41" W 90"

The pouch-equipped bills and large size of **PELICANS** are distinctive.

The **BROWN PELICAN** is strictly a bird of the coast. These birds gather in southern California and in Mexico to nest. The brownish young are on the wing in June and July when they, along with their white-headed parents, disperse. Many move northward to spend the remainder of the summer and fall along the California and Oregon coasts. A few individuals drift as far as the Strait of Juan de Fuca and to Vancouver Island. From the time of their first appearance until the end of November, Brown Pelicans can be seen over the ocean or in the bays and river mouths where concentrations up to a hundred or more are occasionally observed. Small fish compose all of their diet. The bird obtains its prey either by spectacularly diving upon it from a height of 25 to 30 feet in the air or by scooping it from the water while positioned on the surface, much like a fisherman wielding a large dipnet from a boat. Securing prey in this latter manner is frequently a group activity, engaged in not only by a number of pelicans, but by cormorants, gulls and terns. Gulls, at such times, harass pelicans into giving up their catch.

The **AMERICAN WHITE PELICAN** is one of America's largest and most spectacular birds. With a wingspan often reaching nine of ten feet, an enormous orange bill and bold black and white plumage these birds can hardly be misidentified. Flocks often climb high in the air to soar and maneuver in unison, the sun flashing brightly on their brilliant plumages. Unlike the coastal Brown Pelican, these birds do not dive for their food but catch it on or near the surface by swimming or wading in the shallows. Feeding flocks often gather over shallow water and with much flapping and splashing push the fish shoreward where they are more easily captured. White Pelicans are summer residents of the large inland lakes, often moving about from one lake to another. Large flocks summer in favored areas but they are rare and erratic breeders in the Northwest. On rare occasions individuals or small flocks will visit westside valleys and coastal areas but seldom linger.

American White Pelican   Summer   *L 50″ W 110″*
A.C. Fisher

Sitting on pilings or sandbars, standing on offshore rocks, or swimming in nearby waters, **CORMORANTS** are a conspicuous form of coastal bird life. They are goose-sized birds, appearing totally black, but with a close view in good light a purple or greenish iridescence can be noted. They are expert fishermen, diving from the surface and swimming under water often to great depths after their prey. Many people believe that cormorants compete with commercial and sport fishermen and reduce their catches. Some authorities claim that these birds help even the aquatic balance by reducing the population of trash fish, thereby increasing the food supply for other species. Cormorants nest in large colonies on off-shore rocky islands, or in smaller groups on ledges and steep cliff faces. on rocky headlands and promontories. They are year-round residents.

Three species of cormorants occur along the coast and in saltwater bays and estuaries. The Double-crested Cormorant also occurs regularly on bodies of fresh water. Young cormorants are similar in appearance to adults, but show more brown in their feathers; the underparts are of a lighter color, often to the point of being white. All species of cormorants are in the habit of standing with the wings partially distended for intermittent periods; occasionally at such times the wings are slowly moved to and fro.

The **PELAGIC CORMORANT** is noticeably smaller and slimmer than other cormorants. During the breeding season it shows white patches on each flank. At this season, in good light, the highly iridescent green sheen of the feathers becomes brilliant. This sheen caused early ornithologists to call this species the "Violet-Green Cormorant." From late summer through winter when the white patches disappear and the sheen is dulled, the smaller size, and sometimes almost serpentine neck, head, and bill will aid in recognition of the Pelagic Cormorant.

Pelagic Cormorant   Summer   Immature   L 22" W 40"

Z. M. Schultz

Brandt's Cormorant   *Summer*   *L 29" W 50"*

The larger **BRANDT'S CORMORANT** has a deep-blue throat pouch not normally distinguishable from the remainder of the bird's plumage. During the breeding season the color of the throat pouch brightens noticeably and is striking. Several long white plumes can be discerned alongside the neck at this time.

The **DOUBLE-CRESTED CORMORANT** is about the same size as the Brandt's Cormorant. The base of the bill and the throat pouch are bright yellow at all seasons and constitute a good field mark. There is little difference from one season to the next in adult plumages, except for a few small tufts of white plumes atop the head in the early breeding season. Double-crested Cormorants also occur on large inland bodies of water, including major rivers. Their nests are built in colonies near marshes and lakes, on tall trees, on matted vegetation, or on islands in the marshes.

Double-crested Cormorant   *Summer*   *L 27" W 50"*

11

Great Blue Heron L 38" W 70"

HERONS, EGRETS, and **BITTERNS** are long-necked, long-legged, wading birds which catch their prey by amazingly quick movements of neck and bill. A variety of animal life is taken, including fish, frogs, insects, and even small birds and mammals. A member of this group can be recognized in flight by the long neck folded back on the shoulders, by the long trailing legs, and by the slow, deep wing beats. The birds appear awkward when taking off and landing. Frequently, a hoarse, gutteral utterance is emitted as the departure occurs. Most of these species have distinctive crests or plumes on the head. When viewed close at hand during the breeding season many individuals show long, thin plumes on the breast and over the back.

The **GREAT BLUE HERON** is one of the largest resident birds, reaching four feet in height. It tends to be a solitary feeder, but where the food supply is abundant, numbers of individuals can be found together. Blue Herons congregate to nest in tops of tall trees in areas protected from strong winds and human disturbance. Several hundred pairs may nest in one heronry, but one or two pairs may be the total in other, apparently less desirable places. Heronries are habitually used year after year until either the trees fall or disturbance by humans drives the birds away. They can be found in a variety of habitats, at the edges of salt-water bays and estuaries, on lakes and ponds, along fresh-water rivers and small streams, in marshes, meadows, and at times, in dry, upland fields where they engage in catching small rodents.

L. B. McQueen

Green-backed Heron   **L 14″ W 25″**

The stocky **GREEN-BACKED HERON** is a lover of secluded boggy places, and of slow-moving, wood-clogged sloughs and ditches. It is seldom seen in the open, and in the Pacific Northwest is a comparatively uncommon bird at any season, particularly in winter. Green-backed Herons are perhaps the most acrobatic of the herons as they feed and climb about the wooded tangles of their chosen haunts. They often dive into the water in pursuit of prey. The Green-backed Heron is a dark colored bird, but in good light shows a chestnut head and neck and bluish-gray body. Immatures are browner, but the size and shape identify them. Green-backed Herons are not communal

True to its name, the **BLACK-CROWNED NIGHT-HERON** is seldom seen in daylight, except when discovered asleep in some dense tree or bush. Feeding areas are similar to those of other herons, being about marshes and at the shallow edges of ponds and rivers. Adults are pale gray and white in color with dark backs. In the breeding season this bird has long white head plumes; strangely, its rather striking plumage does not render it particularly noticeable. Immature night-herons are brown with whitish spots scattered over the entire plumage. They are often mistaken for the marsh-loving American Bittern, but are duller in color, and without contrast in pattern.

Black-crowned Night-Heron   Immature   Adult   **L 20″ W 44″**

Z. M. Schultz

Great Egret
L 32" W 55"

Snowy Egret
L 20" W 38"

The gleaming white **GREAT EGRET** is almost as large as the Great Blue Heron, but it is more slender. Almost exterminated by plume hunters at the turn of the century, the Great Egret has increased greatly in number under protection. They can be recognized by size, color, the black legs, and heavy yellow bill. The smaller, black-billed **SNOWY EGRET** is rarely noted in the Northwest, although small numbers breed in southeastern Oregon and northern California.

The stocky, yellow-billed **CATTLE EGRET** is increasing in numbers in southern states. Wandering individuals are occasionally seen in fall and winter in the region covered by this book.

Cattle Egret   *Immature*   L 17" W 37"

14

American Bittern

Z. M. Schultz
L 23″ W 45″

The secretive **AMERICAN BITTERN** is a heron of the marshes and of wet, brushy meadows. These solitary birds are experts at the art of camouflage. They show no plumes or bright feathers. They habitually freeze with neck and bill pointed to the sky, and remain in that position as long as they think themselves unobserved. While they are in this pose the brownish-streaked plumage melts into the shadowy depths of the cattails and sedges. In the spring and summer the strange call notes of this bird are frequently likened to the sound of a distant pile driver "oong-ka-choonk." This betrays its presence. The birds nest on a platform of marsh plants, deep in the marsh. These solitary birds never gather into colonies or flocks.

The exotic **WHITE-FACED IBIS** is only a rare fall wanderer over most of the Northwest. Those wishing to observe these splendid birds must visit the Malheur National Wildlife Refuge where a thriving colony nests in the marsh near the headquarters. They can regularly be seen feeding in the meadows or flying to and from their nests. At close range the rich chestnut, greenish and violet glosses can be seen on their plumages; however, from any distance these birds appear uniformly blackish. Size, coloration, and the heavy down-curved bill make these birds readily recognizable.

White-faced Ibis   *Adult Summer*   L 19″ W 37″
15   Z. M. Schultz

Sandhill Crane

L. B. McQueen
L 37" W 80"

The stately **SANDHILL CRANE** is a shy inhabitant of open fields and grasslands. It is usually impossible to approach closely enough to observe the reddish forehead, but the large size and the shape of the bird are adequate for certain identification. The Sandhill Crane is often mistaken for a Great Blue Heron, but the former's browner coloration, its more stately demeanor and the fluff of feathers in place of a tail will separate the two. The outstretched neck and legs in flight give cranes an appearance much different from the hunched-up look of the herons; a labored downbeat of the wings and a quick flick on the upbeat is typical of the crane's manner of flight. The Sandhill Cranes' resonant "gar-ooo" can be heard for over a mile, causing the birds to be heard long before they are seen.

They are gregarious and seldom occur singly, even during the nesting season. During the summer months Sandhill Cranes scatter about the extensive marshlands and wet meadows east of the Cascade Mountains to nest and raise their young. A few pairs nest each year in Pitt Meadows, east of Vancouver, British Columbia. Migrating birds schedule stops at many regular feeding and resting areas east of the Cascade Mountains. Individuals migrating west of the Cascades pass southward through the Puget Sound-Willamette Valley Trough, seldom stopping until they reach Sauvie Island and the Ridgefield National Wildlife Refuge at the confluence of the Willamette and Columbia Rivers. Most continue on to their wintering quarters in California, but a few remain to winter each year. Away from the regular nesting and feeding areas Sandhill Cranes are rarely observed.

L. B. McQueen

Mute Swan   *L 40"*

The large, white, heavy-bodied **SWANS** feed in the shallows, using their long necks to reach underwater plant life. They rarely graze on grasses, but wild swans sometimes visit cornfields and other upland wet farmlands in search of seeds and roots. They use their large webbed feet to dig out and loosen roots and bulbs, often leaving the feeding grounds in ruins. In shallow ponds their style of feeding leaves craters, at times six feet across and two feet deep, quite noticeable when the water recedes in shallow fresh-water bodies.

The European **MUTE SWAN** has been imported to grace many park ponds and country estates in North America. It is hardy, and sometimes small groups become semi-wild. On British Columbia's Vancouver Island several hundred Mute Swans live in the wild and occasionally visit mainland points in the northern Puget Sound area. Adults have an orange bill with a large black knob on its base; young birds' bills are pinkish, turning to black at the face. The neck is usually held curved in an arch with the bill tilted downward. This typical posture differs from the native Tundra and Trumpeter Swans which carry their black bills horizontally and hold their necks stiffly erect. Mute Swans are not totally silent but can grunt a few barking sounds; they will hiss violently when disturbed or annoyed. In flight a loud rhythmic throbbing is made by the wings.

The **TUNDRA SWAN** nests in northern Alaska and Canada. These birds move southward in October, seldom stopping until they reach their wintering grounds. They were rare west of the Cascades until complete protection was given them. Since then they have increased greatly and are apparently continuing to do so. Injured birds are often captured and brought into city parks and zoos for care and recovery. Good numbers of Tundra Swans can now be observed on favored wintering grounds in the Fraser River Delta, along the lower Columbia River, and in parts of the Willamette Valley. Smaller wintering numbers occur along the coast and through the Puget Sound lowlands. Large migratory concentrations often occur on the large wildlife refuges east of the Cascades. Swans mate for life and family groups usually remain together through the winter.

By early March Tundra Swans move northward, but migrants from further south continue to pass through even during May. With gleaming, snow-white plumage and large size, these swans stand out in drab winter countryside like no other bird. Immature birds are grayish white, but are otherwise quite similar to adults. Many adult individuals show a diagnostic yellow spot near the base of the black bill ahead of the eye, but not all birds show this mark. Clamorous in flight, they are for the most part silent while on the water. A flock passing over sound like geese, except that the notes are mellower or more musical. Long whoops and "wow" notes are heard, interspersed with hooting "who-who-who" calls.

On the brink of extinction not many years ago, the **TRUMPETER SWAN** has staged a remarkable comeback under careful protection. It is by no means an abundant bird, but it continues to increase. Prior to the advance of civilization, Trumpeter Swans wintered in company with the much more abundant Tundra Swans on the lower Columbia River, and with less frequency, in Puget Sound and the Willamette Valley. Recent winters have brought a return of a few individuals to their ancestral wintering grounds. They usually occur in family groups among the much more abundant Tundra Swans or in smaller flocks of their own. Introduced breeding populations are permanent residents in some sections east of the Cascades. Although for the most part larger and heavier, with distinctly heavier heads and bills, Trumpeters cannot safely be separated in the field from Tundra Swans on these points alone.

The all black bill and stiffnecked carriage distinguishes adult Trumpeters from Mute Swans, but from black-billed Tundras the voice is distinctive. A loud, sharp tone given singly or in a series while in flight, in quality like a French horn, is much different from any other swan or goose call. Unfortunately Trumpeters seldom call. Suspected Trumpeters thus must often go unconfirmed. Immature Trumpeter Swans are grayish, like other immature swans; however, they show yellowish colored legs and feet. If seen, this point will distinguish this species from the others which show gray or blackish feet and legs. The bill of immatures is pinkish as in the other two swans, but is dark both at the base and at the tip.

Tundra Swan   L 36" W 85"

Trumpeter Swan   L 45" W 95"

Although smaller and more somberly dressed than swans, the four species of **GEESE** which occur regularly are much better known and beloved. There is no difference in the appearance of male and female geese; immatures are similar in appearance to the adults. Geese mate for life and staunchly protect their nests and young. They are instinctively wary and highly intelligent birds, characteristics which enabled geese to maintain good population levels even in the days of market hunting. Today they provide the basis of an active and prolonged hunting season. Many people have heard and seen geese in migration; to many, the sound drifting down from V-shaped flocks high overhead heralds the changing of the seasons. The honking calls of geese differ somewhat in each species, and with a little practice geese can be identified by voice alone. In their feeding habits, most geese are much given to grazing on land, though they also feed in shallow water after the manner of swans. Geese consume a great deal of insect and aquatic life when it is readily available.

The abundant and well-known **CANADA GOOSE** nests from Siberia across North America to Labrador and southward through the Great Basin to California and Colorado. Large numbers spend the winter in the Pacific Coast States where available food in farm fields and wildlife refuges renders wintering feasible. Canada Geese are easily domesticated, and when allowed to return to the wild they frequently remain in the release area as semi-permanent residents. Extremely clannish, those individual Canada Geese which nest together also winter together, resulting in each isolated population differing somewhat from other populations. Because of this, Canada Geese vary in size from that of a duck to a swan, and vary in color from very dark to quite light. The honking call notes vary somewhat in distinct populations also. Regardless of size or color, a Canada Goose can always be identified by its black head and neck on which is imposed a broad white cheek and throat patch.

The primary food of the medium-sized **BRANT** is eelgrass. Large flocks winter in bays and estuaries where this plant abounds. Otherwise, they are found only in passage. Seldom to they stray from salt water. Migration takes place over the ocean, usually just offshore. Flying in single file, long lines can occasionally be seen just off the beaches in spring and fall. If watched closely these lines can be seen to undulate up and down and from side to side as each bird in turn follows the leader as the flock proceeds on its way. They are among the few birds that deliberately migrate in the face of strong winds and heavy storms; they appear to take delight in the challenge. In appearance, they are similar to Canada Geese, with shorter necks from which the black coloration extends through the belly. They ride higher in the water and show much more white under the tail than do Canada Geese. They do not have white cheeks, but have some white on the neck. Pacific Brant are distinguishable from the Brant of the Atlantic Coast by their black bellies; the eastern bird is black only through the breast, and has a white belly. Very seldom are Brant found in domestication.

Z. M. Schultz

Canada Goose   L 16"-25" W 50"-68"

Brant   L 17" W 48"
Z. M. Schultz

The fall migration of the **GREATER WHITE-FRONTED GOOSE** follows a rather narrow and direct route to its wintering grounds in California. Gathering in the north, the main flight appears along the Washington Coast in late September. In the vicinity of the Columbia River, or a bit further south, this movement turns inland and crosses the Cascades to Klamath Basin and Warner Valley. Their flight path takes many birds directly over downtown Portland, where their laughlike "wah-wah-wah" call notes are sometimes heard on fall evenings. Seldom do they stop, except when weather conditions unfavorable to completion of the flight are encountered. In some years spectacular migrations are noted when this species, along with Snow Geese and Alaskan races of Canada Geese occur simultaneously in passage.

In March and April the northward movement of geese is more leisurely, with many stops for food and rest. Even at this time, White-fronts are not frequently observed on the ground as they often stop by night and migrate by day. White-fronted Geese appear quite gray from a distance, resembling some domestic geese, a fact they apparently realize, as sometimes a weak, crippled or sick bird recuperates among a farm flock. Close up, the white patch about the bill and on some birds the black-splotched belly are distinctive. In flight the plain over-all coloration and speckled-belly along with the bird's distinctive voice will help in recognizing this species.

The white **SNOW GOOSE** is often mistaken for a swan. The smaller size, shorter neck, and bold, black wing tips are distinctive identification characteristics for the Snow Goose. Rusty coloration in irregular pattern is often observed on the face and head, and at times on the breast. Young birds are grayish with dark bills. Although a few individual Snow Geese may sometimes be found among resting or feeding flocks of other species of geese, they prefer to remain in flocks of their own kind. From a distance these flocks look like snow-flecked fields or shore edges. All white domestic geese do not show black wing tips or the distinctive black "grin" patch on the bill. Breeding in Siberia and Arctic Canada, Snow Geese move southward on a broad front and are consequently more widely seen than the White-fronted Goose. Major wintering areas are in the Central Valley of California and the Skagit River Delta of Washington. There seems to be a fairly regular interchange of birds between these two distant wintering grounds throughout the season, so that flights can be noted at intervening points almost anytime during the winter moving north or south. The high pitched musical honking calls are sometimes heard from so high in the sky that the birds can't be seen.

Spectacular concentrations gather on the Great Basin refuges in Southeastern Oregon and Northeastern California during migration each season; Summer Lake and Lower Klamath Refuges are the most favored. Among these flocks can often be seen the rare mallard sized **ROSS' GOOSE** (not illustrated), an almost identical duplicate of the larger Snow Goose. Its stubby bill does not show the "grin patch" of the Snow Goose.

L. B. McQueen

Greater White-fronted Goose *Adult*   *Immature*   *L 20″ W 60″*

Snow Goose   *L 19″ W 59″*
Z. M. Schultz

The **DUCKS** differ from swans and geese in several ways. The male of each species shows a brilliant, well-marked breeding dress with readily apparent identifying marks. Females are duller and show few bright markings. Immature plumages are usually quite similar to the adult female. During the mid-summer molt, when ducks cannot fly, the bright males molt into a drab, female-like "eclipse" plumage. This they retain until their flight feathers are replaced. Surprisingly, the well-known "quack" calls associated with many ducks are given by the female. Male ducks of most species tend to be silent and give only low grunts or whistling notes. Although all ducks can dive if need be, one group does not make a habit of doing so and feeds by tipping up or grazing on land. The members of this group are commonly called surface-feeding or puddle ducks and though primarily vegetarians, they will also take aquatic life for food. The diving ducks, on the other hand, frequent larger bodies of water, presumably because the members of this group need to run along the water to become airborne, and since they dive for their food, can catch their prey in deep water. This group is often also referred to as sea or bay ducks, but individuals often occur on inland bodies of water. Many species in this group resort to large inland marshes for their nesting activities.

The **MALLARD** is probably the best known of all ducks. This highly adaptable species can adjust to almost any waterfowl or food supply situation. They domesticate easily, so that many farm or park flocks of ducks contain Mallards or individuals which show indications of Mallard antecedents. They are common permanent resident and breeding birds throughout the Northwest. Migrant birds from northern nesting grounds arrive in winter to bolster local numbers and to contribute to hunting season success. Primarily a ground nester, the Mallard has been known to nest on broad tree branches and on man-made structures off the ground. Like all puddle ducks, Mallards feed either in shallow water or on dry land. They are uncommon on salt water, and are seldom seen on bays and inlets, but they do occur in marshy areas where coastal rivers enter salt-water bays. In flight the Mallard appears as a heavy duck. Males are gray birds having dark heads and breasts with a white ring about the neck.

At close range, and in good light, the male head is a beautiful iridescent green and the breast is rich chestnut. Females have a bluish speculum or patch on the trailing edge of the wings which is bordered by white. Occasionally there is noted among domestic flocks or in the wild a bird which appears to be a very dark female Mallard with a straw-colored head. This would be the **AMERICAN BLACK DUCK** (not illustrated) introduced from eastern North America. The rather dull speculum shows no white borders. The sexes are alike. It is a saltmarsh bird as well as a bird of fresh water.

Mallard   ♀   ♂

Z. M. Schultz
L 16" W 36"

The medium-sized **GADWALL** is not as brightly plumaged as other puddle ducks. From a distance the male appears plain gray or grayish brown with a very noticeable black rump. Females are similar to female Mallards, but are smaller and trimmer. In flight the pure white speculum is easily seen against the darker wings. Shallow, slow-moving streams and marsh ponds are preferred over more open water. Gadwall are often found in small groups away from other ducks. They are uncommon migrants and winter residents in the Northwest. A few nest west of the Cascades, but the marshes of the Great Basin provide nesting habitat for large numbers of Gadwall.

Gadwall   ♂   below   ♀   above   L 14½" W 35"

Z. M. Schultz

The elegant **NORTHERN PINTAIL** is an abundant migrant and winter resident. The comparatively long neck and pointed tail provide a silhouette which is particularly distinctive for this gray and white duck. The female shows an iridescent brown speculum, with white trailing edge, has a less pointed tail than the male, but does have the same elongated neck. Large flights of dull-colored juveniles and eclipse-plumaged adults occur in August and September along the coast. Were it not for the characteristic silhouettes of the birds comprising these flocks, they would be hard to identify. Later as the adults molt into their winter plumage, identification becomes easier. Pintail are common breeding birds of the large marshes east of the Cascades. Elsewhere they are not regularly seen in summer.

The **GREEN-WINGED TEAL** is another of the puddle ducks which winters abundantly in the Northwest. It prefers marshy, weed-choked bottoms or wooded sloughs where the birds are hard to see. Many are seen in fall among feeding shorebirds on shallow ponds and wet mudflats, both inland and at coastal localities. Here they sift food from the muddy bottom or pick plant life from the edges. Later, when excessive water fills these pools, the birds resort to the marshes and flooded meadows. The small size and bright green speculum is distinctive in all plumages. The Green-winged Teal is active on land, and is often seen walking rapidly over farm fields or into pond-side woods in search of food. A few scattered pairs remain in the Northwest to nest each year.

The marsh loving **BLUE-WINGED TEAL** is a rather uncommon summer resident throughout the Northwest. Since 1950 this small, dark-colored duck has become more regular in occurrence in Western Washington and Oregon than it previously had been. It is partial to grassy marshes providing heavy cover. Blue-winged Teal can be seen most often during migration when they associate with other ducks in more open situations. Strictly a fresh-water bird, it rarely visits coastal bays or estuaries. A few individuals are observed each winter, particularly at the time of the popular Christmas Bird Counts, but most migrate to the south long before winter sets in. The small size and large blue wing patches which appear conspicuously in flight are sufficient to identify Blue-winged Teal from all other ducks other than the Cinnamon Teal. The white crescent on the face of the male is distinctive and can often be noted even in flight. The female cannot be distinguished in the field from the Cinnamon Teal, nor can the two species be separated when in the eclipse plumage.

Z. M. Schultz
Northern Pintail ♀ ♂ L 18½″ W 35″

Z. M. Schultz
Green-winged Teal ♀ ♂ L 10½″ W 24″

Blue-winged Teal ♂ ♀ L 11″ W 24″
Z. M. Schultz

The rich plumage of the male **CINNAMON TEAL** is distinctive. All other plumages of this species are indistinguishable from that of the female Blue-winged Teal. The large blue patch on the upper side of the wings will separate both sexes of these two species from all other species except the considerably larger Shoveler. Both Blue-winged and Cinnamon Teal have similar habits, and appear in the same marshy habitats. Both have become more regular west of the Cascade Mountains in recent decades; the Cinnamon is recorded more frequently. Cinnamon Teal are rarely observed in winter in our region but the first returning birds appear as early as February.

The **EURASIAN WIGEON** is one of the most abundant and popular game birds on the Eurasian Continent. It is never observed in any numbers in the Western Hemisphere, but individuals occur each winter among flocks of the closely related American Wigeon. The general plumage pattern of both species is similar, but in this species the body is gray rather than brown and the head is rusty rather than whitish or speckled brown. The female shows a somewhat browner head than does the female American Wigeon, but in the field they cannot be easily separated. The wigeon's love of grazing on grass brings it to city parks and golf courses during the winter months. Here the flocks can be scanned at close range and the Eurasian picked out. It is amazing how the bright and distinctive males can avoid being conspicuous. The two species of wigeon are so similar in habits that what is said of one applies to the other.

The abundant **AMERICAN WIGEON** is the most conspicuous wintering duck along the Pacific Coast. Great flocks are regularly observed resting in farm fields, rafting on coastal bays or inland lakes, or grazing on the grass in urban parks and golf courses. The musical "whew-whew" notes of the male can be heard constantly from a flock. The female's "quack" is more subdued. The male has large white patches on the upperside of the wings, a brown body, a grayish-brown head with a bold green patch through the eye, and a snowy white forehead. Female wigeon have some of the white in the wings and show more brown on the sides of the body. The early fall flights from the nesting grounds are made up of rather somber-plumaged immatures and eclipse-plumaged adults. Although the white wing-patches are considerably reduced at this time, they still can be discerned; that, and the voice of the male birds will help in recognition.

   Wigeon are fond of many of the sub-surface salt-water plants and are frequently seen among feeding Brant, Canvasback and other diving ducks. If wigeon cannot reach food by tipping, they will rob the diving ducks, snatching plants from the victims' bills as the divers emerge. American Wigeon are uncommon breeding birds of the Great Basin marshes and a few may summer throughout the Northwest and may attempt to nest in proper habitats. Wigeon are seldom found in domestic flocks, but wild birds readily come to a regular grain supply.

American Wigeon   ♀   ♂   L 14″ W 34″
Z. M. Schultz

Z. M. Schultz
Eurasian Wigeon   L 13½″ W 32″

Cinnamon Teal   ♂   ♀   L 11″ W 25″

The medium-sized **NORTHERN SHOVELER** is a regular breeding bird of the Great Basin marshes. It may attempt nesting in proper habitat elsewhere in the Northwest but is seldom seen at that time of year away from the preferred marshes. It is a regular but usually not abundant migrant and winter resident, mostly west of the Cascades. The Shoveler's large spoonbill is used to strain food from the surface of the water. Shovelers prefer shallow, almost stagnant, fresh-water ponds where animal life and seeds can float on the surface. They often stir up the muddy bottom with their feet, but seldom do they tip like other puddle ducks to reach down with their bills. They are easily recognized by their out-sized bills and in flight by the large bluish wing-patches. The males in breeding dress are colorful, with iridescent green heads and chestnut sides. The white breast is not as showy as in the Pintail.

The male **WOOD DUCK** is one of the most beautiful of the world's birds. The female is much more subdued in pattern and plumage, but also shows distinctive markings, including a thin crest on the head. They seldom occur in open situations in the wild; their proper habitat is small ponds or wood-clogged, slow-moving sloughs. In these situations the birds usually are seen when they are flushed from along the dark edges and make away from the observer. As they fly off they appear as all dark birds with rather long, broad, square-tipped tails.

The distinctive "creek-creek-creek" notes of the female and "peet-peet-peet" calls of the males will be enough to name them Wood Ducks. On the water, they are delightfully different from any other duck. Nesting as they do in natural cavities in trees or in woodpecker holes, these birds suffered greatly when the forests were cleared and woodlots thinned. Their numbers have increased tremendously in recent years with the addition of artificial nesting sites in the form of boxes provided for their use. Wood Ducks are now common summer residents and nesting birds throughout the region. A few remain to winter in protected freshwater pockets.

The **REDHEAD** is typical of the diving duck group. The males show solid patches of color and the females are a rather plain grayish-brown. The puffy, round, dark head and grayish white sides and back will distinguish the male of this species from other divers. The reddish head is obscure in poor light. Females are similar to females of other diving ducks but show little of the face markings noted on the others. The Redhead is a true diver, seldom seen on land; it must patter for some distance across the surface of the water to become airborne. This species is rather rare in our region, except for a sizeable breeding population in the Klamath and Malheur Basins and lesser numbers in other large marshes in Southern Oregon and Northern California. Redheads may occur singly or in small groups in migration or during the winter months on any large open body of fresh or salt water. Redheads are usually found associating with other diving ducks, particularly scaup, but close examination will separate them.

Northern Shoveler ♀ ♂

L 14" W 31"

Wood Duck ♂ ♀

L 13½" W 28"

Redhead ♀ ♂ L 14½" W 33"

The **RING-NECKED DUCK** is a diving duck of marsh-bordered ponds and sloughs. It is almost never seen on salt water and seldom occurs with other diving ducks; it prefers small groups of its own kind. Ring-necked Ducks are fairly common migrants and winter residents in our region, and appear regularly on city ponds. A very few are found in summer on the high mountain lakes nesting in boggy spots about the edges. In dark, closed-in places frequented by these birds the best distinguishing mark on the male is the pure white crescent at the side in front of the wing. The female is grayish-brown with a white eye-line and a diffused white patch about the base of the bill. Both sexes have two light rings around the bill.

The Eurasian **TUFTED DUCK** (not illustrated) is a very rare visitor to North America. When it has been found, it has almost always been among closely related Ring-necked Ducks, from which the Tufted Duck can be recognized by the long, loose crest on both sexes. Males have all-white sides and show no crescent before the wing. Only one ring occurs on the bill.

The **CANVASBACK** is one of the more distinctive diving ducks. The sloping forehead, chestnut head and neck, and highly visible white back and sides distinguish the male at any distance. Females have the same recognizable profile as the males, differing from them only in a duller color. Canvasbacks are the most highly prized of all the game ducks. Unfortunately, unstable water conditions on nesting grounds and overshooting in the past have caused a marked reduction in numbers. Low bag limits, and in some years complete protection, have not caused a resurgence in numbers. Nonetheless, the Canvasback can be found regularly in winter on coastal bays and estuaries along the West Coast. This is another of the species often found with Brant and other ducks on eelgrass beds in coastal bays where Canvasbacks often inadvertently provide food for thieving coots and wigeons. Small numbers of Canvasbacks occur also in winter on large, fresh-water lakes where they feed on wapato and other water plants. They are uncommon summer residents and breeding birds in many of the favored waterfowl marshes of the Great Basin.

The **GREATER SCAUP** is a common migrant and winter resident on saltwater bays and estuaries. Smaller numbers visit large fresh-water lakes and rivers if those bodies are deep and are rich in plant life. Small numbers of nonbreeding birds remain in summer on the larger bays and on Puget Sound. This species and the closely related Lesser Scaup are difficult to distinguish under most circumstances. The male Greater Scaup is slightly larger, has a whiter back and a more rounded head. The white wing-stripe on the Greater Scaup extends into the primaries, much farther than on the Lesser Scaup. This is the most reliable difference between the two species. The brownish females are otherwise indistinguishable in the field.

Z. M. Schultz

Ring-necked Duck ♀ ♂ L 12″ W 28″

Z. M. Schultz

Canvasback ♀ ♂ L 15″ W 34″

Greater Scaup ♂ ♀ L 13″ W 31″

Z. M. Schultz

The **LESSER SCAUP** occurs as a common migrant and winter resident on large bodies of both fresh and salt water. A few remain to summer, mostly with the Greater Scaup on saltwater bays. Fair numbers nest in many of the Great Basin marshes. This species is more likely to occur on fresh water than is the Greater Scaup, but the rule is by no means infallible. Both species are found on salt water in about equal numbers. Lesser Scaup are somewhat smaller than the Greater Scaup and are grayer on the back. The wing stripe in this species is shorter than on the Greater; no white appears on the primaries. Scaup are excellent divers and obtain their food on the bottom of deep bodies of water, gathering plant and animal life in areas reached by few other ducks.

The **COMMON GOLDENEYE** is a regularly occurring migrant and winter resident on saltwater bays and estuaries. Good numbers also winter along the Spokane River and on the Turnbull Wildlife Refuge in Eastern Washington. Small numbers may visit other freshwater ponds, lakes and rivers elsewhere. The male is all white with black-appearing head, back and rump. The round, white spot below the eye helps to distinguish this species from the Barrow's Goldeneye, which is considerably less common. Female goldeneyes are gray-bodied birds with rounded brown heads set upon short, white necks. Common Goldeneye are rarely encountered either alone or in tight flocks, but where one is found there are usually others scattered over the same body of water, more or less in proximity to one another. Goldeneye are expert divers and consume a greater percentage of animal life than most ducks. Crabs and other crustaceans are basic winter food. Most are taken by turning over underwater stones and plants.

The tree-nesting **BARROW'S GOLDENEYE** is a seldom observed summer resident and breeding bird about forested lakes and ponds at higher elevations. During the winter months, Barrow's Goldeneye are fairly common in Puget Sound, and occur regularly along the Spokane River and on the Turnbull Wildlife Refuge. Elsewhere in the Northwest they are extremely rare and irregular migrants. The two species of male goldeneye are similar in appearance, but the Barrow's has more black coloring above and has a crescent-shaped rather than circular white spot between the eye and the bill. The head shapes differ between the species, as reference to illustrations will show; but for that, the females cannot safely be separated. Insects form a large part of the diet of Barrow's Goldeneye on the breeding grounds. Crawfish and other crustaceans are also taken, along with small amounts of water plants. Both species of goldeneye nest in natural cavities in the trees or in woodpecker and squirrel holes. The downy young can jump safely from the nest to the ground, even from considerable heights.

Z. M. Schultz

Lesser Scaup   ♂   ♀   L 12″ W 29″

Z. M. Schultz

Common Goldeneye   ♂   ♀   L 13″ W 31″

Barrow's Goldeneye   ♂   ♀   L 13″ W 31″

Z. M. Schultz

The perky **BUFFLEHEAD** is a common migrant and winter resident on both fresh and salt water. It has been seen a few times during the summer on Cascade Mountain lakes. Small numbers of non-breeding birds remain on saltwater during the summer months. The Bufflehead is an expert diver and swims underwater with dexterity. Unlike most diving ducks, this species can rise easily from the surface without the usual running across the water. The black-and-white male Bufflehead is readily identified. The female is also rather easy to recognize by its small size and white head-patch, though the over-eager observer may confuse it at times with the Hooded Merganser. Bufflehead are closely related to the goldeneyes, and like them nest in trees near mountain lakes. Bufflehead feed on insects, crustaceans and other animal life.

The ocean-loving **OLDSQUAW** differs from other ducks by having distinct summer and winter plumages in both sexes. Summer males are dark ducks with a distinct white face patch. The female at all seasons and males in winter can be recognized by the whitish head with dark patches on the cheek and crown. Males in all plumages have elongated central tail feathers similar to those of the Pintail. Immature Oldsquaws are plain brownish-gray ducks showing no distinct markings or wing patches. An aid to identification of Oldsquaw when plumage details are not apparent is the smaller head and bill in comparison to other ducks. They are expert divers and have been known to reach depths well in excess of fifty feet. They are very active feeders and spend more time under water than above while obtaining crustaceans and other animal life. Oldsquaw are regular winter residents south to the northern sections of Puget Sound. South of there they are uncommon, usually occurring individually or in small groups. This species is at rare intervals noted on small fresh-water ponds away from the coast.

The **HARLEQUIN DUCK** seeks out turbulent waters for its winter and summer home. Here the birds feed by diving to the rocky bottom and picking small bits of animal life from beneath the rocks and ledges. This they are said to do while walking along the bottom against the current. At times, they are found feeding in the shallows like a puddle duck. During much of the year along the northern Pacific Coast Harlequins occur on salt water in areas of strong currents. The surf breaking over and about offshore stacks and rocks attracts this species, as do strong tides surging over rocky shallows in bays and estuaries. During the breeding season most Harlequins retire to swift mountain streams where they nest among streamside rocks or fallen trees. They are quite agile on land. Soon after the eggs are laid, the male returns to the wintering grounds, leaving the female to raise the young. At closer range, the striking plumage of the male is readily recognized. From a distance or in poor light, the male appears as an all-dark bird with white markings on the face and in front of the wing. The female is often mistaken for a female Surf Scoter, but it is smaller and has a less conspicuous bill.

Z. M. Schultz

Bufflehead   ♂   ♀   L 10″ W 24″

Z. M. Schultz

Oldsquaw   ♀   ♂   L 15″ W 30″

Harlequin Duck   ♂   ♀   L 12″ W 26″

Z. M. Schultz

L. B. McQueen

White-winged Scoter ♀ *flying* ♂ *L 16″ W 38″*

The **WHITE-WINGED SCOTER** is the largest of the three west coast scoters. The male appears all black while sitting on the water, showing only a small white eye mark, and usually . . . but not always . . . some sign of the white wing patch. The large, curiously swollen bill is not so colorful or distinctive as are the bills of the other two scoters. The brownish-black female at rest sometimes has two whitish spots on the head, and also usually shows some indication of the white wing-patch. The wing-patch on both males and females is always prominent when the birds are in flight.

The only other all-black water bird with a white wing-patch is the Pigeon Guillemot, which is smaller and has a differently shaped, smaller bill. White-winged and Surf Scoters nest in interior Canada, and winter commonly along both the Atlantic and Pacific Coasts. Great flocks of scoters are often noted in spring and fall migration over the surf or rafting in protected coves. Nonbreeding birds remain on the ocean, and in estuaries all summer. White-winged Scoters feed on animal life found on the bottom and cause some concern among oystermen when diving about oyster beds. Individual birds sometimes occur in winter or during migration on large bodies of fresh water.

Surf Scoter ♂ ♀ *L 14" W 33"*

The adult male **SURF SCOTER** is a black duck with prominent white head-patches . . . one on the forehead and the other on the back of the head and nape. This bird's large, brightly-colored bill is unique. The female Surf Scoter is a dark brown bird similar to the female White-winged Scoter, but does not show white wing patches. Females have two suffused white patches on each side of the face; occasionally there is a whitish patch on the back of the head. Females do not have the male's odd bill. Juvenile birds look like females. Scoters have no eclipse plumage as such.

The male Surf Scoter sheds its white head-patches in late summer and for a time is completely black. At this time the bright red and white bill is diagnostic. The wings of an adult Surf Scoter, particularly when the bird is taking off or landing, make a whistling noise which can be heard for a long distance on a windless day. While Surf Scoters often raft with White-winged Scoters on protected waters, they are partial to diving and swimming in strong surf and in off-shore tide rips. Large numbers of Surf Scoters often raft on the open ocean in the most severe sea and wind conditions. They take much of their food from the ocean floor below the breaking surf. Surf Scoters are the most abundant scoter along the Pacific Coast, and even in the breeding season non-breeding individuals can be noted on salt water. Individuals occasionally visit inland lakes and ponds, but the species is quite uncommon away from salt water.

Black Scoter   ♀   ♂   *L 14" W 33"*

The **BLACK SCOTER** swims with its head held high and the bill carried horizontally or slightly elevated. Other species of scoters carry the head lower with the bill tipped down. The coal-colored male Black Scoter is completely without pattern or lighter coloration except for a bright yellow knob at the base of its bill. This feature should be noted for certain recognition of this species, since White-winged Scoters at a distance appear all black at times. The female Black Scoter is similar to other female scoters, but has a whitish cheek and foreneck, superficially like that of the smaller Ruddy Duck. Other scoters show light patches on the side of the head. Black Scoters may occur anywhere on the open coast and may raft with other scoters in bays and estuaries, but in our region they are uncommon for the most part. The strong tidal-surges about the mouths of bays, and the heaving surf around sea stacks and rocks are where to look for Black Scoters and where, at times, they may congregate in groups. This species feeds almost entirely on mollusks and other forms of animal life, gathering them from reefs and submerged rocks and gravel.

| | | | | Z. M. Schultz |
| Ruddy Duck | ♂ | | ♀ | L 11"W 23" |

The chunky male **RUDDY DUCK** is the dandy of the bird world in its summer plumage. Its electric blue bill and chestnut body are well worn by this pompous little egotist. The bright plumage changes to a dark brown in winter when the bill turns blackish; only the white cheek-patch remains. The female and immature plumages resemble the winter male, but a dark streak discernible at close range passes through the white cheek patch. There is no regular eclipse plumage in this species. These sprightly little divers spend much of their time on deep, freshwater ponds and on lakes bordered by weeds, marshes and cattails. In winter many move to the coast to raft with other diving birds in protected lakes and bays.

The spring courtship display is spectacular. Ruddy Ducks walk with difficulty on land and build their nests in marshes or bogs adjacent to open water where, unlike most other ducks, the male remains close by to assist his mate in rearing the young. Ruddy Ducks are abundant migrants and winter residents in our region. They are common about the Great Basin marshes in summer. A few remain west of the Cascade Mountains each year to nest, and are rather easy to observe on the ponds so favored.

The male **HOODED MERGANSER** ranks with the Wood Duck as one of the world's most beautiful waterbirds. His fan-shape crest can be raised or lowered at will, but is always noticeable. The grayish-brown female can be recognized by its bushy crest and merganser bill. Both sexes of this smallest of the mergansers show a white speculum in flight. The bills of mergansers are thin cylinders edged with tooth-like serrations, an aid in holding slippery prey. Hooded Mergansers feed on fish and other animal life found in fresh-water ponds and streams. They often associate with Wood Ducks and share many of that species' habits. Both nest in natural cavities in trees and readily use artificial nest boxes. The young of both species leave the nest by clambering to the opening and dropping to the ground, where the mother is waiting to lead them to the nearest water.

Hooded Mergansers seem to prefer fewer obstructions in the water than Wood Ducks do, and often utilize faster-moving streams, where Wood Ducks would be decidely out of place. Hooded Mergansers flush directly from the water and are quite agile on land; both are characteristics they do not share with other mergansers. Hooded Mergansers are fairly regular but secretive permanent residents of the Pacific Northwest. They occur mostly on freshwater streams, on small ponds, or at the edges of undergrowth along the shores of larger ponds.

The bold **COMMON MERGANSER** prefers large, open lakes and rivers. The long-bodied black-and-white males with their red feet and bills are distinctive. The reddish-brown of the crested head and upper neck of the female is sharply separated from the white of the lower neck. On the otherwise similar female Red-breasted Merganser, the reddish-brown of the head and neck merges with the white of the lower neck by blending. In flight, a merganser's head, body and tail make a straight line, giving the bird the appearance of an arrow cutting through the air. Mergansers all are swift flyers. In winter when sunlight flashes brightly from male Common Mergansers, they can be seen for a considerable distance.

Common Mergansers are regular migrants and are common winter residents on fresh water. This species scatters in summer northward and to the interior to nest along larger mountain rivers and about large wooded lakes. They are rare in our region at that season. The birds nest in trees when suitable cavities can be obtained, or on the ground if necessary. The Common Merganser is an accomplished diver and strong swimmer, but is clumsy on land and in becoming airborne. Its diet is comprised largely of fish, mostly slower-moving non-game species. In impoundments where trout or other game fish abound, Common Mergansers take their share, thereby drawing the ire of fishermen and hatcherymen.

Hooded Merganser ♀ ♂ Z. M. Schultz L 13″ W 26″

Common Merganser ♂ ♀ L 18″ W 37″
Z. M. Schultz

The **RED-BREASTED MERGANSER** is a common migrant and winter resident of the saltwater bays and estuaries of the northern Pacific Coast. Occasionally individuals or small groups visit freshwater lakes and rivers, but they are quite irregular away from salt water. This species nests in the far north where breeders and non-breeders alike spend the summer months. They are almost never seen in our region in June or July. The first fall migrants appear in August and September. The primary food of this species, too, is fish. In its winter home it seldom has the opportunity to feed on concentrated game fish and for the most part relies on rough fish to meet its needs. Red-breasted Mergansers are rapid swimmers and active divers, and regularly fish in the surf and about offshore rocks. The male lacks the white sides of the Common Merganser; it shows a double-pointed crest and a and a rusty band across the breast at the waterline. Female Red-breasted Mergansers can, with a little practice, be distinguished from female Common Mergansers. In the former, the brownish color of the head and upper neck blends to the white of the lower neck and breast; whereas, in the latter species, there is a sharp line of demarcation between the colors.

Red-breasted Merganser ♀ ♂ L 16" W 33"

Z. M. Schultz

44

Z. M. Schultz

Turkey Vulture
L 25" W 72"

The **TURKEY VULTURE** or turkey buzzard frequents open farm, range, and sparsely forested areas where its glider-like flight seems effortless. Vultures rely on air currents to keep them airborne and once aloft they seldom flap their wings. On the ground the situation is reversed. Only with great effort and deliberation do they succeed in becoming airborne. Food is exclusively carrion, and they are more likely to occur in livestock areas.

Turkey Vultures are most plentiful in warmer, drier areas but are regularly found throughout the Northwest during the summer months. These birds are quite conspicuous migrants and are among the first to return in the spring. Turkey Vultures use communal roosting sites which are usually in groves of tall trees. Good launching sites are essential. They assemble at roosts late in the afternoon and don't move out in the morning until the air is sufficiently warm to create updrafts. When perched, Turkey Vultures often face the sun and extend their wings in a drooping manner.

In flight the upturned wings and small head provide a distinct silhouette, and from the underside, the outer and trailing portions of the wing are much lighter in color than the forward portions. On the ground or perched, the large size and small naked head are distinctive.

VULTURES, HAWKS and **FALCONS** are diurnal birds of prey that live mostly on the flesh of other animals. All, except the vultures, prefer to catch their prey alive, but many turn to scavenging when hunting is poor.

The birds of prey that commonly occur in the Northwest fall into six distinct groups: Vultures, Accipiters, Buteos, Osprey, Harriers, and Falcons. Each group is rather distinctive in its habits and mode of hunting, but because of size and plumage variations among each group, species identification is often quite difficult.

Plumages among these birds tend toward patterns of browns, grays and white. The female is usually larger and more aggressive than the male. Taking live food places them at the top of the food chain and makes them highly susceptible to the effects of pesticides and other harmful pollutants concentrated in the bodies of their prey.

Northern Goshawk   L 19" W 42"   adult   immature

Z. M. Schultz

R. B. Horsfall

Sharp-shinned Hawk L 10½" W 21"
Cooper's Hawk L 15½" W 28"

COOPER'S and **SHARP-SHINNED HAWKS** are included in the accipiter group. These are bird-eating hawks which dart from seclusion to catch unwary prey. They often operate around bird feeders, but usually all we see of them is a flash of blue or brown. Small birds keep constant watch for these two hawks which, like other accipiters, have long tails and short, stubby wings which alternate between flapping and soaring. Sharp-shinned Hawks are small (10-14") and have a square-tipped tail as opposed to the larger (14-20") Cooper's Hawk which has a round-tipped tail. Separating these two is difficult for even an experienced observer, especially since female hawks are larger than males. Also, sizes overlap and color varies between brown and gray. The nests of these hawks are difficult to find for they use dense growth of conifers.

The **NORTHERN GOSHAWK** is the largest and boldest of the accipiter, or bird hawks. Living in the wildest, most heavily forested areas it is seldom observed by man. Its large size allows it to hunt grouse, ducks and other large prey. In extreme weather Goshawks are forced to find food in the lowland valleys. It is then that it becomes a "chicken hawk," and a scourge of the farmyard. In the distinctive gray plumage of the adults it is easily identifiable, but the brownish immatures are very similar to the Cooper's and Sharp-shinned Hawks. Large female Cooper's Hawks often overlap male Goshawks making identification even more difficult.

The resident **RED-TAILED HAWK** is the most common and wide-spread of the buteo or broad-winged hawks. This group hunts by soaring over open fields or sitting on exposed perches, dropping down on small mammals, such as mice or squirrels. Large insects are also eaten when available. Because of their conspicuous mode of hunting, buteo hawks are often accused of being 'chicken hawks' around farming areas; in reality, buteos seldom feed on birds. The accipiters, or 'bird hawks' hiding in a nearby woods and swooping down on the farmyard and returning to the protection of cover are the usual culprits. Buteo nests are bulky piles of sticks placed in trees or on cliff faces. They are used and built up year after year until many become enormous.

A large hawk sitting on a telephone pole or in a tree showing a dark head and conspicuous white breast will most likely be a Red-tailed Hawk. The bright red tail of the adult is diagnostic but many immatures in dark or unusual plumages cannot be safely identified.

The **ROUGH-LEGGED HAWK** is slightly larger and longer winged than a Red-tailed Hawk but shows the typical shape of this group. It is a winter visitor from the north that joins the Red-tails in their taste for mice and squirrels, but prefer treeless prairies and more open farmlands and meadows. They are often seen sitting on the ground or hovering on slowly beating wings scanning the land below for movement. When perched the paler head shows little contrast with the light breast, but the very dark, solid belly patch is quite notice-able. In flight, the long broad wings are very light when seen from below with a conspicuous black patch at the 'wrist'. The light col-ored tail is crossed by a broad black band that often covers the terminal half.

Red-tailed
Hawk
L 18″ W 48″
(left)

American
Kestrel ♂
L 8½″ W 21″
(right)

R. B. Horsfall

48

A.C. Fisher

Rough-legged Hawk
L 19" W 52"

The **AMERICAN KESTREL** is the most abundant and widespread of the falcon group. Falcons have distinctive silhouettes, long pointed wings and long tails. They are built for speed and agility. The larger species are attracted to ducks, grouse and other large prey, while the smaller species pounce on sparrows, mice and insects. All but the Kestrel are decidedly uncommon and seldom seen. The larger species nest on cliff faces, while Merlins and Kestrels use large woodpecker holes or other tree cavities.

The colorful American Kestrel is most often seen perched high over open fields or meadowlands on utility poles or wires searching with their keen eyesight for their prey to present themselves. They frequently hover on updrafts or on beating wings ready to pounce on anything seen below. Kestrels often visit large city residential areas in winter in search of House Sparrows and small mice. Most, however, remain about farming areas. They are easily recognized by their small size, falcon shape, and distinctive facial markings.

A.C. Fisher

Swainson's Hawk
L 18" W 49"

The **SWAINSON'S HAWK** is a buteo of the dry prairies east of the Cascade Mountains. They are uncommon but widespread summer residents that migrate southward in fall to winter in Argentina. Occasional migrants are reported west of the Cascades, and a small number may even summer on the San Juan and Gulf Islands in the 'rain shadow' of Vancouver Island.

Swainson's Hawks are similar in appearance and habits to immature Red-tailed Hawks and are difficult to separate. Many adults often show a distinctive dark wash across the breast that contrasts a bit with the lighter underparts, the opposite pattern usually seen on a Red-tailed Hawk. All Swainson's Hawks can be identified in flight by the underwing pattern: the primaries and rear half of the wing are very dark, often contrasting with the lighter forewing, a feature not found on the Red-tailed or other Northwest buteo hawk.

The beautiful **FERRUGINOUS HAWK** is a rather rare summer resident of the open rangelands of the Great Basin Country east of the Cascade Mountains, reaching into Southeastern Washington. This large 'squirrel hawk' has very white underparts and a clear white tail usually washed lightly above with rufous. The head and upper parts are rather light also. Often the adult's rufous 'leggings' can be noticed as they pass overhead.

Modern land use practices have reduced the populations of many prairie loving birds in the Northwest. Both the Swainson's and the Ferruginus Hawks have been affected.

Ferruginous Hawk   L 20" W 54"

The spectacular **PRAIRIE FALCON** is the 'bird hawk' of the prairies, occasionally visiting the lowlands west of the Cascades. Rapidly passing over sagebrush or meadow, this dusty colored large falcon easily obtains birds often as large as doves and quail. The falcon shape, light coloration, and especially the distinctive black patches at the base of the underwing identifies this species.

Prairie Falcon
L 16" W 40"

51

Merlin   L 12" W 23"

The **MERLIN** or Pigeon Hawk, hardly larger than the diminutive Kestrel, is the falcon of open woodlots and hedgerows. It is an uncommon winter visitor throughout the Northwest. The few that remain to nest are rarely observed. It is a rather dark bird in shades of brown and gray. It does not show the reddish brown coloration or the strong facial markings of the Kestrel.

The great **PEREGRINE FALCON** or Duck Hawk is the favorite of falconers for its speed and agility. It can pursue and overtake teal and other ducks in full all-out flight. Its primary food is waterbirds and, when observed, it is in areas where these birds gather. Almost as large as a crow, the falcon shape and heavy facial markings will identify it. It is a rare winter visitor over all of the Northwest. A few breed in favored areas, especially along the British Columbia Coast.

The **NORTHERN HARRIER** is a slim, long winged hawk of meadows, farm fields and coastal dunelands. A medium sized hawk gliding and flapping in a zigzag or undulating fashion low over fields is likely to be a Harrier. Its habit of holding its wings above the horizon when gliding and its bold white rump patch are good field points. Some adult males are so nearly white that they can be mistaken for gulls. Harriers feed largely on mice but occasionally take small birds. They nest on the ground.

Peregrine Falcon
L 15″ W 40″

Northern Harrier L 16½″ W 42″ ♂ and ♀ (right)

The powerful **GOLDEN EAGLE** preys mostly on rabbits and similar sized rodents, floating on set wings high overhead using its keen eyesight to spot activity below. A swoop low over the ground and the rabbit is secured in the vice-like grip of the eagle's talons. An adult Golden Eagle is a large dark colored hawk showing little contrasting color other than a subdued golden wash on its head and shoulders. Immatures are similar but show conspicuous white patches at the base of the tail and in the wings.

This species is most often seen in the dry sagebrush country east of the Cascade Mountains and occasionally about large dry meadowlands and open mountainous areas where cliff face nesting sites are available. A few regularly visit the Willamette Valley and the Gulf and San Juan Islands, especially in winter.

The majestic **BALD EAGLE** is one of the largest birds of prey. It is primarily a fish eater but may take any animal life readily available. A fish idling on the surface may become prey for a swooping Bald Eagle, but most are taken dead or dying on the beaches or tidal flats. Bald Eagles also harry Ospreys and other birds for their catch. Sick or injured waterfowl are a wintertime source of food about refuges or other places where waterfowl concentrate. Bald Eagles also follow salmon to their spawning grounds to feed on the dying fish. A few Bald Eagles occur each winter in the Willamette Valley where they feed on dead sheep and other domestic animals. The birds are often accused of killing these animals, but careful observation has indicated that the eagles find them already dead. Bald Eagles are wary and require relatively secluded areas for nesting and feeding. Human disturbance is a major cause of their disappearance in many areas. The adult Bald Eagle is unmistakable but the dark immature can be confusing. During the four years required for immatures to acquire the distinctive adult plumage, they may show indistinct patches of whitish anywhere on the body. Most show a whitish area along the fore portion of the under wing. The similar Golden Eagle has definite white patches on the tail and under wings and the fore portion of its under wing is always dark.

Bald Eagles are common residents in coastal British Columbia south to northern Vancouver Island and to a lesser extent are present throughout the Gulf and San Juan Islands. Further south, Bald Eagles occur as isolated pairs about coastal bays, along larger rivers, and around some of the larger lakes. Migrants move southward to winter about favored feeding grounds. The largest winter-time concentrations in our region occur around Puget Sound, along the lower Columbia River, and especially in the Klamath Basin where several hundred gather every year.

Golden Eagle   adult
L 32" W 78"

Bald Eagle   adult   immature flying   L 32" W 80"

Z. M. Schultz

Osprey   L 22" W 54"

The long-winged **OSPREY** is often mistaken for an eagle. It shows a
large amount of white about the head and over most of the underparts. The wings are held with a distinct crook of the "wrist" in
flight. The food of Ospreys consists entirely of fish which the birds
catch by cruising over a body of water until prey is spotted near the
surface; the birds then hover briefly on beating wings before plunging feet first into the water to grasp the prey in their talons. Bald
Eagles often watch for an opportunity to rob Ospreys laboring with a
freshly caught fish. The Osprey is an uncommon summer resident
and breeding bird throughout the Northwest. It occurs in isolated
pairs about many large bodies of water or along fair-sized streams. In
particularly favored areas, Osprey gather in loose colonies and are
rather common. Ospreys are partial to fresh water, but also regularly
occur about bays and river mouths. Occasionally an individual will
winter in our region, but it is usual for Ospreys to migrate south by
November, returning in February and March.

Z. M. Schultz

Sage Grouse   ♂   ♀
L 22″

The spectacular **SAGE GROUSE** is a bird of the sagebrush country east of the Cascade Mountains. They are most common in the Great Basin becoming less regular to the north and west. During early spring Sage Grouse gather in early mornings on established dancing grounds, or "leks," to perform their elaborate courtship displays. Here, the males raise and spread their pointed tail feathers and inflate large air sacs, hidden below the white breast feathers. With their wings held low they strut about, occasionally releasing air from the sac to produce a loud "plopping" noise.

Any pheasant-like bird, almost as large as a Turkey and showing a bold black belly patch, can be safely noted as a Sage Grouse.

The similar, but much smaller **SHARP-TAILED GROUSE** (not illustrated) once was widespread in the vast grasslands east of the Cascade Mountains. Remnant populations still gather at "leks" in a few remote localities but the species cannot cope with civilization and is disappearing rapidly. Ring-necked Pheasants are often mistaken for Sharp-tailed Grouse but the grouse has a shorter, white edged tail.

The familiar **WILD TURKEY** (not illustrated) has been introduced in many sections of the Northwest and has successfully taken hold in several areas. Wild Turkeys are quite similar to their barnyard cousins but are more slender, long-legged, and shy. They are rarely observed even where they are most common in North-central Oregon and Central Washington.

Blue Grouse ♂ *L 17"*
♀ *(below)*

Ruffled Grouse L 14"

The **BLUE GROUSE** is an uncommon resident of the coniferous forests throughout the Northwest. When whirring off from underfoot it can be recognized by its dusky or grayish coloration and dark colored tail. The very low "hooting" calls of the "hooter grouse" is a regular sound of the spring coniferous forest.

The similar **SPRUCE GROUSE** (not illustrated), or "fool hen," is a tame grouse of remote coniferous forests of British Columbia, Eastern Washington, and Northeastern Oregon. It can be identified by the white spots and streaks on its flanks and tail.

The **RUFFED GROUSE** prefers dense deciduous groves and open woodlands, visiting conifers for shade and cover. The drumming noise, produced by its wings, is often heard in foothill woodlots adjacent to open farmlands in spring. When flushed, Ruffed Grouse appear gray-brown showing a black band near the tip of the pale tail.

WHITE-TAILED PTARMIGAN (not illustrated), the grouse of the high alpine country, are pure white in winter and change to brownish in summer. In both plumages it shows a pure white tail. White-tailed Ptarmigan are native southward to the peaks of the Washington Cascades, and have been introduced in the Wallowa Mountains of Northeast Oregon.

The introduced **NORTHERN BOBWHITE,** the quail of Eastern North America, has been established in many agricultural areas in the Northwest. It does not do well and numbers fluctuate greatly. The distinctive facial pattern, lack of a topknot, and the whistled "bob, bob white" call notes identify the Bobwhite.

Mountain Quail L 9"
California Quail   L 8"
R. B. Horsfall

The **CALIFORNIA QUAIL** may not be native to all of the Northwest but it has been widely introduced and now occurs in all open brush and farmland areas. The male has a topknot which tips forward, the female's plume is much shorter. Females are much grayer than the blue-gray males.

California Quail occur most of the year in flocks called coveys. In spring the coveys break up for nesting. Like the pheasant, they are not as abundant as formerly because of the elimination of brush in our farm areas. Brush is essential to them for escape cover and shelter. They feed on waste grain and seeds and are non-migratory.

The male California Quail, especially in spring, gives a single whistled call or three bright notes which sound like "er, er, errr," with the last note slurring downward. The middle note is sometimes higher than the other two.

The similar **MOUNTAIN QUAIL** inhabits burned-over timberlands, brush and patches of second growth timber. They are most common in the drier, more open sections. They are becoming scarcer in more settled, cultivated lands. They can be distinguished from the California Quail by a topknot of long straight plumes, not tipped forward. The sexes are identical.

Northern Bobwhite   L 9"

Z. M. Schultz

Many species of upland birds have been introduced to fill habitats not utilized by native birds; most have failed. The obvious exceptions are the Chukar, the Gray or Hungarian Partridge, and the Ring-necked Pheasant.

The rock-loving **CHUKAR** inhabits steep barren hillsides and cliff faces in the dry uncultivated lands east of the Cascades where few other birds can survive. The face pattern, red legs, and bold chestnut and white slashes on its flanks identify this species. Their loud cackling calls can often be heard on still days, far out from their hillside lookout posts.

The **GRAY PARTRIDGE** has established itself about irrigated farm-lands, mostly east of the Cascades, especially in the Columbia Basin. Introductions west of the Cascades have not done well. Gray Part-ridge are recognized by the orange face and rusty "horseshoe" on its underparts. In flight the rusty tail is a good field mark.

The **RING-NECKED PHEASANT,** commonly called "China pheas-ant," is familiar to nearly everyone. The hen is plain brownish gray in contrast to the brightly spangled cock. This bird is not a native but was first introduced near Albany, Oregon, from China in 1881 by Judge Owen Denny. This was the first successful U.S. introduction of this popular game bird. However, in recent years Ring-necked Pheasants have declined drastically. Wildlife biologists correlate this with the conversion of small farms with much fence cover to large fields without cover along the edges. Ring-necked Pheasants occasionally live in urban areas where there is an abundance of brush and open space.

Ring-necked Pheasants are polygamous. A cock usually has a harem of several hens. Despite being ground dwellers and poor fliers, they often roost in Douglas firs. The crowing of the Ring-necked Pheasant reaches a peak in the spring. An explosion or sonic boom will trigger a crow.

Ring-necked Pheasant   L 27"   ♂

R. B. Horsfall

Z. M. Schultz

Chukar
L 10"

Gray Partridge
L 10"

Z. M. Schultz

Virginia Rail

Z. M. Schultz
L 7½" W 14"

The elusive **VIRGINIA RAIL** is a denizen of bogs and swampy places where the vegetation is lush and thick. It is a master of concealment and can slip through the thick cover with scarcely a ripple to indicate its movements. Rails seldom leave the heavy cover and rarely flush, but when they do, the birds make off on fluttery wings with legs dangling, going only a short distance before dropping into the marsh again. The strange, piglike grunts and "kid-ick" calls of Virginia Rails are often the only indication that a marsh contains any of these interesting birds. Virginia Rails and Soras are often found together and both rely on small animal life and seeds for food. The Virginia Rail, however, will occupy shallow drainage ditches and small roadside wet patches more readily than the Sora. Virginia Rails are regular summer residents and breeding birds throughout the Northwest, even to the high mountain meadows and slightly brackish coastal marshes. They scatter widely in late summer and many migrate southward. They are silent for the most part during the winter and are seldom encountered then although they may be fairly regular winter residents in lowland marshes.

Sora

L. B. McQueen
L 6¾" W 12½"

The chicken-like **SORA** may be more common than the Virginia Rail, but it is less often seen. It prefers more extensive areas of marshland or bog and seldom can be flushed or pushed into the open. Soras are noisy birds, so the marsh home of the Sora is seldom a quiet place during the breeding season. The most common calls are mild peeping notes; its loud "whinny" is the strangest and most distinctive of the many calls of this species. Tape-recorded rail calls are useful for luring these birds into openings in the sedges or cattails. When seen during the summer months rails are often accompanied by their black downy young. Immature Soras do not show the black face-patch of the adult and are browner. Soras are regular summer residents and breeding birds in the lowland marshes and wet high-grass meadows. They seldom occur in the higher elevations, except in migration. They are rarely observed in winter in our region.

A diverse group of small to medium-sized birds utilize the food supply found in wet mud, sand, on rocks and in shallow water. These birds can be recognized by their medium long legs and fairly long bills. They are generally referred to as **SANDPIPERS** or **SHOREBIRDS.** The smaller species have come to be referred to by birders as "peep." At one time shorebirds were eagerly taken for food and were sold on the open market. Many were considered fine game birds. They are so easily killed and their reproduction rate is so slow that they had to be placed under complete protection to keep them from becoming extinct. Today only the Common Snipe is on the game bird list. As a group, the shorebirds are among the world's greatest travelers and many can be observed as they pass between their winter and summer homes. From late June to November and in April and May large flocks of shorebirds may be observed in favored feeding areas on their way through the Northwest.

Most of the shorebirds have a bright, summer plumage that changes to a plain, more obscure wintertime camouflage dress. In many species loud distinctive call notes can be used for identification. Shorebirds are extremely gregarious and gather into large flocks, often comprised of several different species. They do not, however, nest in colonies. Since each species is adapted for acquiring food from a particular source, considerable variation occurs among the different forms. In learning to identify the shorebirds, it is helpful to organize the different species into unofficial groupings by similarity in habits or by preference for the same habitat. For instance, the plovers seldom wade in water, but run about in mud or upland flats or on grasslands, stopping suddenly to pick a bit of food off the ground. By comparison, the numerous "peeps" are generally found in large flocks scattered over the flats or wading in shallow water while probing for their food. Rock-loving species of shorebirds often flock together to glean their food from surf-washed rocks or from pebble beaches. Phalaropes are swimming birds which pick their food from the surface of the water. The large-sized, long-billed shorebirds can be placed in still another group.

The chisel-billed **AMERICAN BLACK OYSTERCATCHER** is a rock-loving shorebird of the Pacific Coast. It's a wild and wary bird, rarely allows close approach by humans. The brightly colored bill is used to pry open various shellfish found in tidal areas. The bird's black plumage blends well with the wet rocks, but the bird is so noisy and active that it often reveals itself to the observer despite its superb camouflage. These large, black birds with bright red bills can hardly be mistaken for anything else. Their vocalizations are also unlike those of any other bird of the Pacific Northwest. Black Oystercatchers are rather uncommon permanent residents on the offshore rocks and rocky headlands along the open ocean. A small number occur in the San Juan and Gulf Islands in northern Puget Sound and the Strait of Georgia. Black Oystercatchers are widespread in summer but gather often into wintertime flocks made up of a score or more individuals. This species seldom mixes with other shorebirds.

American Black Oystercatcher

Z. M. Schultz
L 15″

The **SEMIPALMATED PLOVER** is the plover of the mudflats. It regularly associates with "peeps" and other shorebirds. The brown backs of Semipalmated Plovers so closely match the color of mud or wet sand that the birds are often overlooked until flushed. They seldom, if ever, wade in the water and usually are to be found on the still damp but drier upper flats and edges. Their "chee-whee" calls can be heard frequently and distinguished readily from other shorebird calls. The single neck-ring and the solid brown back distinguish this species from the other plovers. Semipalmated Plovers are common migrants along the coast and are fairly common inland. A few remain both to summer and to winter on attractant coastal flats.

Semipalmated Plover

L 5¾″
Z. M. Schultz

Snowy Plover   Summer   Winter   Z. M. Schultz   L 5¼"

The pale **SNOWY PLOVER** is the plover of the dry sand dunes and alkali flats. Along the coast it finds the dunes and upper tidelines to its liking, feeding on insects and flies generated by decaying material in the sea wrack at the tideline and on whatever small animal life presents itself in the dunes. Inland, the Snowy Plover finds sand dunes and abundant food about the many alkali flats and lakes east of the Cascade Mountains. In both areas they nest on the dry sand, seldom making a nest but placing the eggs right on the ground. They often allow the wind to cover the eggs with drifting sand. Snowy Plovers are plump, sparrow-sized birds adorned by an incomplete chest band. In winter they lose most of even that marking, and are quite plain. The dry sand-colored back is distinctive in all plumages. This plover is so well disguised in harmony with its chosen surroundings that it is usually unseen until it runs off in front of the observer. Snowy Plovers are rather rare summer residents and breeding birds along the open beaches and spits north at least to Copalis, Washington. Inland populations are restricted to alkaline areas of Eastern Oregon, but suitable sites occur in Eastern Washington and have been checked out by possible breeding individuals. Most migrate southward in winter, but some remain in favored coastal areas. Ever increasing human activity along the sandy coastal beaches which are its home seriously threatens the future of this species along the coast. Inland areas are more remote but are equally fragile.

Killdeer

Z. M. Schultz

L 8″

The vociferous **KILLDEER** is the plover of upland meadows, farm field, and extensive grassy areas. It is regularly found well into the cities on golf courses and large lawns. It also occurs in more typical shorebird habitats on mud flats and shore edges. The Killdeer nests directly on bare ground, usually where it is gravelly or littered. The birds regularly nest on dirt roads or on gravel edges of lightly traveled rural thoroughfares. In built-up areas Killdeer have been found nesting on flat, gravel roofs. Although the eggs are well camouflaged, the parents often give away their secret by becoming highly excited, emitting their "kill-dee" alarm notes and going into a spectacular broken-wing act. Killdeer are Robin-sized shorebirds with two black neck bands and a golden rump patch. They are common permanent residents, paired and widespread in the nesting season, but gathering into often large flocks in winter. Killdeer seem to prefer fresh water, so seldom occur in concentration on the salt-water flats.

The beautiful **LESSER GOLDEN-PLOVER** in our region is usually found in migration on plowed fields or on short-grass meadows in close proximity to the coast; tidal *salicornia* marshes are also visited. The Golden-Plover is similar in appearance to the larger Black-bellied Plover. In summer plumage, which is seldom observed in the Northwest, the golden-spangled back and underparts, which are black to the tail, distinguish the Golden-Plover from the paler-backed Black-bellied Plover. The fall and winter plumage is very similar to the Black-bellied Plover's; the all-dark back, wings and tail in flight are quite different from the more patterned appearance of the larger Black-bellied. The Golden-Plover at all seasons lacks the black axillars of the Black-bellied.

The Lesser Golden-Plover travels a tremendous distance in its migration. It breeds on the Arctic tundra and passes southward to the southern half of South America as far as the prairies of southern Argentina and to many of the islands in the South Pacific. Birds which breed in Siberia presumably account for the birds which spend the non-breeding season in India, southern China, Australia and the South Pacific. The migration is primarily offshore, but birds occur each fall regularly on coastal flats and more rarely inland. Lesser Golden-Plovers seem to have increased in occurrence along the west coast of North America since 1960, but there is considerable fluctuation in numbers of migrants which occur from one year to another. Birds are observed much more often in fall than in spring, as the spring migration is taken over another route. Occasionally non-breeding birds are seen in summer.

The stocky **BLACK-BELLIED PLOVER** shows considerably more contrast in coloration than does the closely related Golden-Plover. In flight the Black-bellied Plover, which is a fairly large shorebird, shows a white rump and wing-stripe; the black axillars (at the base of the underwing next to the body) can usually be discerned on flying individuals. In summer the back is light gray and the underparts are black only to the legs. The undertail area is always pure white. The mournful "chur-whee" of the Black-bellied Plover is one of the common bird sounds on coastal shorebird flats. This species is somewhat wild and is definitely wary. Its rapid forward movement and quick stop with a brief wait all help to identify the Black-bellied Plover even when it is at a considerable distance. Black-bellied Plovers are rather common migrants in both spring and fall along the ocean coasts where they occur individially or in small, widely-scattered flocks. Large flocks of a hundred or more can be seen in migration on the tidal flats of Willapa Bay and in Grays Harbor. In fact, Black-bellied Plovers can usually be seen in those and other especially favored places the year around. Inland they are somewhat rare but do occur, usually in company with other migrant shorebirds.

Lesser Golden Plover   Summer   Winter   Z. M. Schultz
L 9″

Black-bellied Plover   Winter in flight   Summer standing   L 9½″
Z. M. Schultz

The calico-patterned **RUDDY TURNSTONE** seeks its food by turning over pebbles. shells, bits of driftwood and other sea wrack to gather the insects or small crustaceans hiding underneath. Occasionally these birds will probe or dig for their food on the tidal flats. Individuals often associate with Black Turnstones on gravel beaches and on surf-washed rocks and jetties. The brilliant summer plumage is unmistakable, but in winter it fades to a pattern similar to that of the Black Turnstone. Both species show the striking, dark-and-white "turnstone" flight pattern in all plumages. The winter Ruddy Turnstone has a somewhat concave breast pattern and light, reddish-yellow legs. The body color is brownish-gray, lighter than the blackish of the more common Black Turnstone. Ruddy Turnstones are regular migrants along the salt-water tidal zones. Small flocks occur on mudflats with other shorebirds and along the tide lines on the open beaches. Individuals winter with the abundant Black Turnstones and occasionally non-breeding birds summer in the Northwest. It is one of the earliest migrants in the fall migration and is often seen by late June.

The **BLACK TURNSTONE** is another of the rock-loving shorebirds found along the intertidal zone. It seldom visits the mudflats or sandy beaches, but for the most part remains on the surf-washed gravel bars, jetties and offshore rocks. Here the birds glean small animal life amidst barnacles and sea weeds. This species is often found in large flocks with other rock-loving species. They all show dark grayish-blue plumages, but the Black Turnstone is the darkest. In flight its bold dark and white "turnstone" pattern will separate this species from all but the similar Ruddy Turnstone. The Black Turnstone is a migrant and winter resident of the ocean coast and about Puget Sound. Early fall migrants appear by late June, so the species is almost a permanent resident in the Pacific Northwest.

The rock-loving **SURFBIRD** is a fairly common migrant and winter resident along the ocean coast and to a lesser extent about the rocky areas of the San Juan Islands. In flocks either solely of their own kind or intermixed with Black Turnstones, they can be observed on jetties and tidal rocks. The rather heavy bill is used to pick small mollusks and barnacles from the wet rocks. Surfbirds are stocky, plover-like shorebirds with black or dark gray backs and chests and white bellies. In flight they can be separated from the other species with which they are commonly associated by the white rump, lower back, and upper tail; turnstones have more white in the wings.

The **ROCK SANDPIPER** (not illustrated) is another denizen of the tide-washed, rocky coast. it often occurs in flocks of turnstones and surfbirds on jetties and offshore rocks. In its dark gray plumage the Rock Sandpiper is similar to those species, but it is somewhat smaller, is less robust, and has a longer bill. In flight it shows little pattern but a light wing stripe and light outer tail feathers. It is a very uncommon migrant and winter resident along the ocean coast and about Puget Sound.

Ruddy Turnstone   Summer   Winter   Z. M. Schultz   L 7″

Surfbird   Winter L 8″   Black Turnstone   Winter L 7″
L. B. McQueen

Common Snipe

Z. M. Schultz
L 9"

The **COMMON SNIPE** is a bird of the grassy bogs and wet meadows. Here it uses its long bill to probe in the soft earth for worms, grubs, and other animal life. Its protective coloration makes the bird hard to see on the ground. It usually freezes until closely approached, then flushes into zigzag flight while emitting distinctive "scaip" calls. It is considered a fine game bird because it so frequently outsmarts the hunter.

The male indulges in spectacular aerial courtship flights in the spring as, high in the air, it circles and dives, causing a "who-who-who" as wind passes through the set tail feathers. The noise can be mistaken for the call of a hiding owl. The nest of the Common Snipe is placed in the center of a clump of grass or sedge in a shallow bog or marsh and is well hidden. Common Snipe are widespread permanent residents throughout the Northwest, occurring individually or in small groups. Large flocks are occasionally found in winter when the birds may concentrate during cold spells in spots where seepage prevents freezing of the ground.

The **WHIMBREL** is a large, brown shorebird with a sizeable down-curved bill. Single individuals or small groups of Whimbrels may be found on tidal mud flats, picking and probing on the drier upper areas. Whimbrels regularly visit sandy beaches and salicornia marshes. They have a loud flight call that can be easily recognized, once learned. The series of high "whee" notes is often heard before the bird can be seen. When a number gather to migrate they fly in "V" formation often noted among geese. Whimbrels are common migrants on salt-water mud flats. They are rare inland. Small numbers occasionally spend both winter and summer in favored feeding areas in the southerly portion of our region.

Long-billed Curlew

Z. M. Schultz

19"

The excitable **LONG-BILLED CURLEW** is an uncommon resident of grassy prairies and meadowlands east of the Cascade Mountains. An approach into its nesting territory will elicit an immediate vociferous response from these wary birds as they dive at and fuss about the intruder. Extensive cultivation and overgrazing has driven this bird from many of its former nesting grounds. A good population nests each year on the Malheur National Wildlife Refuge near Burns. A few are observed in migration west of the Cascades each year and occasionally one will linger at some coastal esturine mud flat.

Long-billed Curlews closely resemble Whimbrels but show no head striping and usually have a much longer bill. The bright cinnamon patches under the open wings and the downcurved bill are distinctive.

Whimbrel

L 14"

Z. M. Schultz

Z. M. Schultz

Willet   Winter   13½"

The showy **WILLET** is a summer resident of the Great Basin marshes. Here it appears as a rather plain marbled grayish-brown bird, usually observed standing on a fence post giving vent to its 'pill-will-willet' calls. In winter it is even plainer in its dress of uniform gray, relieved only by being paler below. It is best identified at any time of year when it flashes its bold black and white wing pattern. In migration many scatter to visit marshes and coastal flats throughout the Northwest. A few winter each year on coastal estuaries.

The long-legged **GREATER YELLOWLEGS** feeds primarily on small fish and other aquatic animal life which it catches by rapidly running about in shallow water. The long, bright-yellow legs identify both Lesser and Greater Yellowlegs from other shorebirds. Both species show almost identical plumages, but the Greater is larger, has a longer, slightly upturned bill and calls a series of loud "wheu" notes. The Greater Yellowlegs is a common migrant along the coast and inland, occurring exclusively about shallow waters on mud flats and tidal beaches. A few remain to winter in some years.

Greater Yellowlegs

Z. M. Schultz
L 11"

The **LESSER YELLOWLEGS** is almost an exact duplicate of the Greater Yellowlegs. The Lesser is a bit more delicate in appearance and has a shorter, thinner, straight bill. Its voice is a single or double mello "wheu" note, usually given in flight. Both species sometimes occur together. In migration Lesser Yellowlegs appear in compact flocks, less often occurring individually among other shorebirds. They are common migrants, but pass through the region rather quickly, seldom lingering. They are more common inland than along the open coast.

Lesser Yellowlegs

L 8¾"
Z. M. Schultz

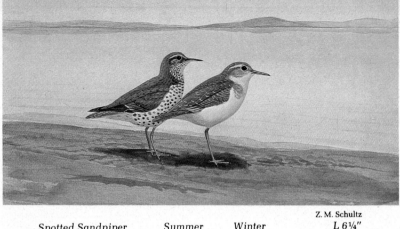

Z. M. Schultz

Spotted Sandpiper   Summer   Winter   L 6¼"

The **SPOTTED SANDPIPER** is a fresh-water shorebird although in winter it frequents tidal areas. It can be recognized by its peculiar habit of bobbing up and down as it forages among and on boulders and driftwood at the edges of mountain ponds and streams. The birds also occur in summer about lowland bodies of water, including the larger rivers of the region. The Spotted Sandpiper flies on stiffly held, arched wings, which are hardly raised above a horizontal position on the up-stroke. As it flies or upon landing it gives vent to a series of "peet-weet" call notes. It is a widespread species and is fairly common during the summer in favorable habitat. Spotted Sandpipers are rarely observed in flocks or associating with other species.

Rarely during the migration season another shorebird occurs in the habitat of the Spotted Sandpiper. This is the **SOLITARY SAND-PIPER.** It can be recognized by its uniformly dark upper parts, its white eye-ring, and its banded tail. It flies swiftly with bold, effortless strokes of the wings, altogether unlike the Spotted Sandpiper.

Solitary Sandpiper   L 7"
Z. M. Schultz

Pectoral Sandpiper

Z. M. Schultz
L 7½"

The erect stance of the medium-sized **PECTORAL SANDPIPER** is often noted among the peep and other shorebirds ranging over open and mud flats. Pectoral Sandpipers are, however, partial to the sparse grass edges and short-grass wet meadows. They freeze in the cover until almost stepped upon, then flush in a zigzag flight loudly emitting "churk" notes. The dark-striped brown plumage on back, head, belly and lower breast are the best field marks. Considerable size variation can be noted among individuals of this species in which the female is noticeably larger than the male. Pectoral Sandpipers are rather uncommon and erratic in their occurrence as fall migrants throughout the Northwest. They appear individually or in small groups; largest numbers are found on coastal salicornia marshes. They are rarely observed during spring in the region.

Occasionally in the fall a bird will appear among Pectoral Sandpipers that shows a more finely striped, buff-colored breast and cinnamon crown. This is the decidedly rare **SHARP-TAILED SANDPIPER.**

Sharp-tailed Sandpiper   *Immature*   L 7"
Z. M. Schultz

Z. M. Schultz

Wandering Tattler   Winter   Summer   L 8¾"

The slate-gray, unpatterned upper parts of the **WANDERING TAT-TLER** make this species rather easy to identify as it works among the rocks or when flying over the water. Its voice is unusually loud and can easily be heard above the roar of the surf. Although individuals or small groups may be observed along jetties or on offshore rocks, they seldom are closely flocked nor associated with other rock-loving shorebirds. Wandering Tattlers are uncommon migrants of the coastal tidal zones; they appear occasionally in Puget Sound. They are noted regularly in summer, but are all but absent in winter.

The bright, buff-brown **BAIRD'S SANDPIPER** shows a distinct scaly pattern on its back. The long wings, extending at rest well beyond the tail, give this species a slim look as it feeds among other shore-birds on the open flats. It usually occurs well away from the water's edge and prefers to feed on the drier flats. In migration Baird's Sand-pipers often stop on the open ocean beaches to feed along the sea-wrack at the high tide line. This species can be easily confused with other peep, but is slightly larger, lighter in color, and has a straight bill. Baird's Sandpipers are uncommon but widespread fall migrants through the Northwest, even to high mountain lakes and snow banks on the prominent peaks of the region. They are rarely observed in spring.

Z. M. Schultz

Red Knot   Summer   Winter   L 9"

The plump **RED KNOT** occurs in close compact flocks in migration, often dropping down briefly upon open ocean beaches to rest. Red Knots are uncommon to rare birds along most of the Northwest coast, but can be found fairly regularly on the shorebird flats in Willapa Bay and about Grays Harbor, where a few may linger in winter and summer. They practically never are to be found away from the coast. This species is often mistaken for a dowitcher or plover. It has a shorter bill than the dowitcher and a thinner, longer bill than the plovers. In breeding plumage, the red breast makes identification easy. At other times, the narrow, white line in the wing and a pale white rump are also good field marks.

Baird's Sandpiper   Adult   Immature   L 6"

Z. M. Schultz

The **WESTERN SANDPIPER** is the most abundant migrant shorebird in the West. From late June to November and again in April and May the tidal mud flats and inland shorelines are alive with peep sandpipers, the majority are this species. Western Sandpipers prefer to feed in shallow water and on very wet mud edges. At low tide they scatter all over the exposed flats; during high tide they often visit grassy areas and salicornia marshes. In the winter months, and in spring, flocks of Western Sandpipers may be found on wet farm fields. The medium-sized bill which noticeably droops near the tip, the black legs and pale breast are good distinguishing points to look for. During much of the year chestnut-colored feathers can be seen on the shoulders and about the head.

Western Sandpipers are abundant migrants in lowland areas throughout the Northwest. Small flocks remain to winter, usually moving about to different areas during the season. The slightly smaller, shorter-billed **SEMIPALMATED SANDPIPER** (not illustrated) is occasionally found among Western Sandpipers; it is almost indistinguishable from them under most conditions, but it lacks the drooping bill and chestnut-colored feathers of the Western.

The **LEAST SANDPIPER** is the smallest North American shorebird. It is usually observed on mud flats, often in company with the Western Sandpiper. The preferred feeding area for this species is further back from the water in the somewhat drier mud and sand. They regularly occur in grassy areas and in salicornia marshes. The small size, dark brown coloration, and dark-streaked breast will separate it from other peep. No other peep-sized shorebird has the yellow legs of this species. Least Sandpipers are common migrants and regular winter residents in lowland salt and fresh-water areas of the region.

The **DUNLIN** is our commonest wintering shorebird and is somewhat larger than the peep. In favored areas Dunlin gather in great flocks, often numbering into the thousands; they sometimes cover the ground like a living blanket. In spring and fall they are to be seen with other migrating shorebirds on the tidal flats and at fresh-water edges; in winter many move into wet farm fields and meadows. The slaty-gray unpatterned back and dusky breast make winter Dunlin rather difficult to identify, but the black patch on the belly and the red back in summer make the species readily distinguishable. The down-curved, rather heavy bill is the sure identification mark for this species in winter. Its somewhat larger size is also apparent when the bird is seen in comparison to other shorebirds with which it is wont to mingle. When Dunlin occur in company with Sanderlings, the Dunlin's dark back makes it quite conspicuous among the paler Sanderlings.

Western Sandpiper   Winter   Summer

L. B. McQueen
L 5¼"

Least Sandpiper   Winter   Summer

Z. M. Schultz
L 4¾"

Dunlin   Summer   Winter   L 7"

Z. M. Schultz

Long-billed Dowitcher   Winter   Summer   Z. M. Schultz   L 10"

The **LONG-BILLED DOWITCHER** is a regular migrant and early winter visitor to soft, wet mud flats and open marshes. In those habitats, it probes, sewing machine-like, often plunging its long bill to the hilt. In addition to their long bills, dowitchers are white on the rump and lower back, a field mark which is readily apparent when the birds fly. In summer plumage the Long-billed Dowitcher shows more barring on the sides of its cinnamon underparts than does the almost identical Short-billed Dowitcher. In winter the two species are really indistinguishable in appearance. However, the voices of the two species are distinctive and can be used to separate them. In the long-billed species a series of "keek" notes is usually heard both when the bird is on the ground and when it flies.

Long-billed Dowitchers are common migrants, appearing on fresh-water mud flats and in farm fields. Small flocks remain through December in favored areas. They are uncommon but regular migrants on salt-water tidal flats, usually in company with the more abundant short-billed species.

The bill of the **SHORT-BILLED DOWITCHER** (not illustrated) is not noticeably shorter than the bill of the Long-billed Dowitcher; it is thus of little aid in distinguishing the two species. The plumages are almost identical and, except when the birds are in breeding plumage and are observed at close range, the appearance of the birds is of no use in recognizing which species is present. Under most circumstances of observation, then, only the difference in voice is distinctive enough to separate the two species. The voice of the Short-billed Dowitcher is similar to that of a yellowlegs, a mellow series of "theu" notes given when flushed and in flight. They are rather silent while feeding, but occasionally give low "to" notes.

The Short-billed Dowitcher is a common migrant on salt-water tidal flats and marshes. The bird is an uncommon and irregular non-breeding summer resident in a few favored coastal areas of the Northwest. Inland and on fresh water the Short-billed Dowitcher is rarely observed, but when it does so occur it is usually among flocks of the long-billed form.

Z. M. Schultz

Marbled Godwit
L 16"

The **MARBLED GODWIT** is a large, long-billed shorebird which feeds on the wet mud flats in a manner similar to that of the dowitchers. The vertical rapid thrusting of the long bill into the soft mud differs considerably from the random probings of the similar-sized Whimbrel. This species is uniformly buff-brown with a flash of cinnamon under the open wings. The chief distinguishing point is the typical godwit bill—long, slightly upturned and noticeably pink on the basal half. Marbled Godwits are uncommon migrants both east and west of the Cascade Mountains, occasionally stopping at wet grassy meadows, but most often observed on bare mud flats or along the open ocean beaches. They are usually observed in small groups, but occasionally large numbers can be seen on particularly attractive feeding grounds. During some winters, small numbers may be seen on the mud flats at Yaquina Bay, Oregon, but they are seldom observed at that season elsewhere in the Northwest. The Asiatic **BAR-TAILED GODWIT** (not illustrated) and the white-rumped **HUDSONIAN GODWIT** (not illustrated) both have been observed on the tidal flats of the Pacific Northwest, but these occurrences have been almost accidental. Both species show the typical godwit bill, but are grayish in color and are more distinctly patterned than is the Marbled Godwit.

The active little **SANDERLING** is the familiar shorebird of the ocean beaches where it vigorously pursues food in the wet sand of the surf line. During most of the year this species is one of the palest of the shorebirds. The only prominent dark mark is a black patch at the bend of the wing. In flight the wings show a white stripe. For a brief period in late spring the adults show a rich rusty wash over much of the body. Sanderlings are abundant migrants and rather common winter and non-breeding summer residents on the ocean beaches, often visiting the tidal mud and sand flats inside the bays and harbors. They are uncommon but regular winter visitors about Puget Sound and up the Columbia River to Portland.

The **RED PHALAROPE** spends almost its entire life on the open ocean well offshore. The birds obtain their food by picking minute crustaceans and other organisms off the surface of the ocean. Like the other phalaropes, this species swims with a distinctive bobbing of the head as they quickly move about. The bright summer plumage, much brighter in the female, allows ready identification of the Red Phalarope. In winter the birds are pale gray with unmarked backs and thick yellow bills; the absence of black stripes on the back aids in distinguishing this species from the winter-plumaged Red-necked Phalarope. Red Phalaropes are common migrants well offshore.

Occasionally an individual or a small group may be seen from a jetty or about the mouth of a river feeding on the tide rip. They are most often seen, however, when strong early winter storms drive migrating birds onto the beaches and into the bays and harbors; occasionally great numbers are found after a severe storm, particularly in November. In some years birds are driven into Puget Sound and the Willamette Valley by such storms. After such occurrences, decreasing numbers may be found at coastal points for weeks and sometimes months later.

The dainty little **RED-NECKED PHALAROPE** is the most common swimming shorebird found west of the Cascade mountains. The needlelike bill and dark, patterned back separates this species from the other phalaropes. The female is the dominant sex in all phalaropes. She shows the brightest plumage and performs the mating displays. Often in spring, a female can be seen bowing and bobbing as it rapidly swims round and round a demure little male, all the while fluttering her wings and softly grunting soft "quet" notes of endearment.

Red-necked Phalaropes are common migrants throughout the west; in our region they are most abundant along the ocean and about Puget Sound. The main migration route is well offshore and coastal movements are often quite erratic, depending apparently on the conditions at sea. Occasionally small numbers remain through much of the winter.

Sanderling   Summer   Winter   Immature

Z. M. Schultz
L 6½″

Red Phalarope   Summer   Winter

Z. M. Schultz
L 6½″

Red-necked Phalarope   Winter   Summer   L 6″

Z. M. Schultz

Wilson's Phalarope   Summer   Winter   Z. M. Schultz
                                                     L 7½"

The lovely **WILSON'S PHALAROPE** is the largest of the phalaropes. In any plumage it can be distinguished in flight from the other swimming shorebirds by its uniformly dark wings and the white rump patch. It is mostly a freshwater species and does much of its feeding on foot about grassy marshes and mud flats. It nests in dense grass meadows. The birds often feed in shallow water by rapidly spinning about to stir up the muddy bottom, then gathering the small animal life which clusters to the surface. Although Wilson's Phalaropes breed in large numbers in the marshes of the Great Basin, they are uncommon migrants and summer residents west of the Cascades. They appear most often there in coastal lowlands and about Puget Sound.

The showy **AMERICAN AVOCET** is a conspicuous summer resident of alkaline flats and shallow pools east of the Cascades. Only rarely is it observed west of the mountains. Like most ground nesting birds, it has perfected a "broken-wing" act and other ruses to lure away an intruder from its nesting territory. It is a loud, aggressive bird without peer in its vicious and vociferous attacks against trespassers. Avocets are often found wading in shallow water picking up food from the bottom of the pool or whipping their long, upcurved bills from side to side on the surface of the water obtaining floating insects. In fall many are attracted to the downwind side of large lakes where windrows of floating insects are cast ashore.

In late summer Avocets lose the cinnamon wash on their head and neck and appear as bright black and white birds.

Black-necked Stilt

Z. M. Schultz
L 13″

The graceful **BLACK-NECKED STILT** is an uncommon summer resident of alkaline waters east of the Cascade Mountains and is seldom noted elsewhere in the Northwest. In these areas they are close companions to the Avocet, where their quiet, stately demeanor is in marked contrast to the latter's loud, aggressive behavior. Apparently aware of their long dainty looking legs, Stilts often perform a "broken leg" act about the nest and present them conspicuously in other showy ruses.

American Avocet   Summer   L 15″
Z. M. Schultz

Glaucous-winged Gull *Adult Winter* *Immature*

Z. M. Schultz
L 22"

The long-winged gray and white **GULLS** are abundant and well-known water birds throughout the west. Of the many species which occur, most can be readily identified with practice, despite their confusing similarity. Identification must be done with care, paying close attention to the coloration of the mantle (back and wings), to the degree of contrast between primaries (the long outer wing feathers) and wing-tips, and the bill and leg colors.

In winter the leg and bill coloration is faded, and the white head and neck are streaked with gray. Black-headed gulls lose their head color and show distinctive dark markings on the head instead. The sexes of gulls are alike in appearance, but there are distinctly different immature plumages. Most gulls indulge in considerable scavenging, both in the wild and about dumps and refuse disposal areas. For this valuable work they are rigidly protected. Gulls are for the most part, highly gregarious, nesting in close colonies and gathering in large flocks to feed and to migrate. Several species may occur together in these flocks.

The large, pink-footed **GLAUCOUS-WINGED GULL** in adult plumage can be identified by the pale gray mantle and dark gray (not black) wing-tips. During the four years it takes the immature to acquire full adult plumage, the birds gradually lighten from mouse-gray to white. The primaries and wing-tips are gray in all plumages. The bill, solid black in the juvenile, slowly lightens from the base. Glaucous-winged Gulls are abundant residents and breeding birds on offshore rocks, headlands and on islands and pilings in bays and harbors from coastal Washington northward and in Puget Sound. A few summer south to the central Oregon coast, occasionally interbreeding with Western Gulls. Glaucous-winged Gulls scatter southward in winter along the coast into California and inland along the larger rivers and about large bodies of water.

Occasionally in winter the large pure-white **GLAUCOUS GULL** (not illustrated) may be seen in a flock of the larger gulls. If the bird shows a pale-colored bill with a distinct black tip, it would certainly be this rather rare visitor from the far north. First winter Glaucous Gulls are speckled brown and white, but still show all white primaries.

Western Gull   Winter   Z. M. Schultz L 21" W 55"

The large, pink-footed **WESTERN GULL** is mostly a saltwater species, although in winter a very few occasionally visit freshwater areas away from the coast. This species has the darkest mantle of all the western gulls. The underwing primaries do not have so much a black patch as a wash of grayish extending well back onto the wing. This shows up well in most conditions. Immature Western Gulls are very dark, brownish-black with black primaries. During the four years it takes the birds to reach maturity, they can be confused with immature Herring Gulls which, however, show more contrast between mantle and the darker wing-tips. During the breeding season Western Gulls habitually rob the nest and young of other species on the nesting rocks. They are abundant residents and breeding birds in habitats similar to the more northerly Glaucous-winged Gull, from Central Washington southward. Small numbers nest among Glaucous-winged Gull colonies to Vancouver Island. In winter, Western Gulls scatter along the coast northward into British Columbia and down into Puget Sound while still occupying their breeding range.

The large, pink-footed **HERRING GULL** has a pale gray mantle with contrasting deep-black wing-tips, which show a few small white spots within the black. In poor light the mantle may appear quite dark, causing the bird to be confused with the Western Gull. In the Herring Gull the underwing is very light, except for the well marked black tips. The heavy bill is yellow, with a red spot near the tip. The bird's eyes are pale colored. In the four years it takes the immatures to reach full adult plumage they are difficult to separate from Western and California immatures. Herring Gulls are abundant migrants and fairly common winter residents. They occur on the larger rivers and on or near salt water.

Herring Gull   Winter   L 20" W 55"
Z. M. Schultz

The medium-sized, pink-footed **THAYER'S GULL** is similar in plumage to the Herring Gull and is difficult to distinguish. It is smaller, being more nearly the size of a California Gull, and has a slim, pale yellow or mottled bill. The eyes are dark. It has a pale mantle but there is much less black on the wing-tips than in the Herring Gull; the wing-tips also show larger white spots and wedges than does the Herring Gull. Very little black appears on the under-wing. Immatures cannot be safely separated under most conditions. Thayer's Gulls are common migrants and winter residents west of the Cascade Mountains, often outnumbering Herring Gulls in many areas.

The medium-sized, greenish-footed **CALIFORNIA GULL** is a rather dark mantled gull with well defined black wing-tips that show two large white patches in the black. In winter the feet turn gray-green and the slender bill fades considerably in color. Immatures are somewhat lighter than Herring and Western Gull immatures; they have a pink bill with a black tip, but under most circumstances are difficult to distinguish from immatures of other species. The California Gull breeds in Great Basin marshes and on islands in the Columbia River and migrates from late June into October towards the coast often proceeding northwesterly as they do so. They are extremely abundant in the Northwest during this period in both fresh and salt water areas, but by November a marked decline in numbers is evident. By late winter few remain in our region, but some non-breeding birds may be seen in spring and early summer, mostly along large rivers and in nearby farmlands.

The medium-sized, yellow-footed **RING-BILLED GULL** is somewhat smaller than the California Gull and considerably lighter mantled. The wing-tips are deep black with less white in them than is true of California Gulls; in fact, fall adult-plumaged Ring-billed Gulls often show no white at all in the black wing-tips. The sharply defined black wing-tips can cause this species to be mistaken for a Kittiwake, which has differently colored legs. At fairly close range adult Ring-billed Gulls can be identified with assurance by the complete black ring around the yellow bill. Immatures are prettily marked brown-and-whitebirds with a black band on the whitish tail. Ring-billed Gulls nest in colonies in the Great Basin marshes, on islands in the Columbia River, and at several coastal estuaries. They join the California Gulls in their migration. They are common migrants and winter residents in the Northwest, in both saltwater and freshwater areas where they are frequently seen on nearby farmlands.

Thayer's Gull   *Winter*

California Gull   *Immature*   *Winter Adult*   *L 17″ W 52″*

Ring-billed Gull   *Immature*   *Adult Winter*   *L 16″ W 49″*

The rather small, greenish-footed **MEW GULL** can be identified by its small size and almost plover-like head and bill. The mantle is variable and may be dark gray in the adult to pure white in certain stages of immature plumage. The white in the black wing-tips is extensive and will aid in identifying the species in flight. Mew Gulls are often found in association with Ring-billed Gulls in city parks, on golf courses and on farm fields. At such times Mew Gulls seem to do a lot more walking about than do the other gulls which are present. Immature Mew Gulls are small-billed, brownish and white patterned little gulls with an indistinct black band on the tail. They show considerably less contrast than immature Ring-billed Gulls. This species is an abundant migrant and winter resident along the coast and about Puget Sound. They are also common up the Columbia River to Portland and occasionally further upstream and in parts of the Willamette Valley.

The **BONAPARTE'S GULL** can be recognized in all plumages by the pale gray mantle with a wedge of white on the outer section of the wings. Its small size, bounding buoyant flight and tern-like habits help to identify it. The black head of summer is replaced in winter with a well-defined black spot behind the eye. The bill is black and the legs are reddish. Immatures show a black tail-band and a brownish w-shaped pattern on the upper wings; otherwise they are similar to winter adults.

Bonaparte's Gulls are common migrants in the Gulf of Georgia and in Puget Sound, where a few winter. Elsewhere in the Northwest they are uncommon, though in November they are regular in occurrence along the Oregon Coast. Occasionally among migrant gulls along the coast and in northern Puget Sound, a gull similar to the Bonaparte's Gull is seen which has a contrasting pattern of black, gray and white triangles in each wing. This is the **SABINE'S GULL** (not illustrated), a fairly regular migrant well offshore, but a decidedly rare bird elsewhere, including close inshore.

The little **FRANKLIN'S GULL** is regularly found in migration with other gulls in northern Puget Sound and occasionally may show up almost anywhere on fresh or salt water in the Northwest from July to November. It is a common summer resident and breeding bird at Malheur National Wildlife Refuge. The Franklin's Gull is similar in size to Bonaparte's Gull, except that it is somewhat longer-winged; it lacks the adult Bonaparte's white wing-triangle, but instead shows the familiar dark-gray mantle and black wing-tips of the larger gulls. The black patch in the wing-tips of the adult is separated from the gray mantle by a narrow white area. In fall and winter adults and young show a dark patch extending around the back of the head from eye to eye. The Franklin's Gull has a medium-sized, dark red bill and legs. Immatures have uniformly dark brown upperparts and clear white underparts, and show a white eye ring.

Mew Gull   Immature   Adult Winter   L. B. McQueen
L 14″ W 42″

Bonaparte's Gull   Adult Summer   Immature   Z. M. Schultz
L 11″ W 32″

Franklin's Gull   Summer   Immature   L 11″ W 35″
L. B. McQueen

Heermann's Gull   Immature   Adult

L. B. McQueen
L 15"

The medium-sized **HEERMANN'S GULL** is one gull which is easy to recognize. Adults are very dark gray with a black tail, tipped with white; they have white heads and red bills, and are altogether quite unlike any other gull. Even in winter when the white head is heavily clouded with dusky, the adults are unmistakable. Immatures are dark gray-brown throughout with a distinctive red bill; occasionally, individuals are seen with conspicuous white patches in the middle of the upper wing surfaces. This species nests in Mexico in spring, and then migrates northward in June and July, spending the summer on saltwater as far north as Vancouver Island and sometimes into Puget Sound. Small numbers remain through December in some years, but this is unusual. Heermann's Gulls habitually rob Brown Pelicans of their catch, and often bully other birds.

Black-legged Kittiwake
Adult   Immature

Z. M. Schultz
L 13½" W 36"

The buoyant flight of the **BLACK-LEGGED KITTIWAKE** is quite noticeable. The adult has a light gray mantle and black wing-tips which show no spots of white. The small, unpatterned yellow bill and black legs serve to distinguish adults of this species from adult Ring-billed Gulls. Immature kittiwakes have a dark collar across the back of the neck; a dark diagonal band across the wing and a black-tipped, square tail also help to identify immature kittiwakes. These birds are found sporadically in small numbers throughout the year about river mouths and just offshore. They are regular but uncommon migrants along the coast. Occasionally they may be seen in the Strait of Juan de Fuca and rarely in Puget Sound.

Common Tern   Summer

Z. M. Schultz
L 14" W 31"

TERNS are graceful, gull-like birds with long, narrow wings, forked tails and pointed bills. They feed by cruising over the water, then diving head first to grasp a sighted fish in their bills. They are regularly harassed by the piratical jaegers into dropping their catch and are accompanied by them on long migratory flights.

The **COMMON TERN** is not really common in the Northwest where it occurs in migration, both in spring and fall. It has a pale mantle with rather dark wing-tips. In winter the black cap retreats to a blackish patch across the back of the head and the red bill turns wholly or partially black. The red legs also fade in brightness. When seen at rest, the Common Tern is a small gull-like bird with the wings extending somewhat beyond the tail. Common Terns may be seen along the ocean coast and in the bays and harbors. They are regular in Puget Sound and in the Gulf of Georgia in late summer, but are rarely observed elsewhere away from the ocean.

The very similar **ARCTIC TERN** (not illustrated) is apparently a regular migrant well offshore and is occasionally observed along the coast. They seldom can be recognized in flight but while perched, the wings and tail appear about even in length, and the underparts and face are a bit grayer than the Common Tern. Arctic Terns often show a distinct white line just below the black cap; in breeding plumage the bills are bright red without any black. This species stands so low to the ground that it appears to be seated. Common Terns stand noticeably higher. In the fall the bill and legs of Arctic Terns are no longer bright red, but have become dark. The silvery wing-tips on the **FORSTER'S TERN** are sufficient to distinguish it from Common and Arctic Terns. In winter the black cap is replaced by two black eye patches, differing from the solid patch across the back of the head of the others. Forster's Terns are common summer residents of the Great Basin marshes and rivers, only occasionally visiting west of the Cascades in migration or during the summer.

Black Tern   Summer   Winter

Z. M. Schultz
L 9" W 35"

The marsh loving **BLACK TERN** differs from other terns by having an all black head and underparts. The back and upper wings are silvery-gray. In winter the black is replaced with white, except for dark patches about the eyes and the back of the head. Some dark flecking often shows on the underparts also.

Black Terns are summer residents about many marsh ponds and lakes east of the Cascades where they are most often observed wheeling over the marshes hawking insects. Small numbers occasionally wander west of the Cascades and to the coast in migration.

Forster's Tern   Summer   L 14" W 30"

Z. M. Schultz

Caspian Tern   Summer

Z. M. Schultz
L 20" W 53"

The gull-sized **CASPIAN TERN** shows all the habits of the smaller terns despite its size. The heavy, bright-red bill and black cap are easily observed. The mantle and wing tips are pale grayish but the underwings are quite dark. The loud, distinctive "ca-arrrrr" flight call is often heard before the bird is seen. Caspian Terns are fairly regular migrants along the ocean coast and in summer frequently visit many of the Northwest's bays and harbors, north to Vancouver Island and into Puget Sound. They breed on sandy islands in Grays Harbor, Willapa Bay, and perhaps in other estuaries. Small numbers also breed along the Columbia River and in the Great Basin marshes east of the Cascade Mountains. They are occasionally observed in other areas during migration.

JAEGERS are gull-like sea birds that follow migrant gulls, terns and other fish-eating birds to rob them of their catch. Their falcon-like flight is swift and exceedingly agile. They obtain their food by watching the feeding flocks until a bird catches a fish or some other morsel, then they rush in and harry the bird until it drops its quarry, which the jaeger then retrieves before it hits the water.

Three species of jaegers occur along the West Coast, all of which are primarily offshore birds. They do, however, occur at times as migrants about bays and harbors and in Puget Sound. In plumages and actions all three species are similar, and under most circumstances are difficult to separate. Jaegers are dark birds which show more or less distinct patches of white in the "wrists" of the wings. Most individuals are white below but occasionally completely dark birds occur. All three species share the characteristics of having elongated central tail feathers, which contribute to a streamlined appearance.

Parasitic Jaeger   *Large Light Phase*   Z. M. Schultz
              Common Tern flying   *Small Dark Phase*   L 16"

The **PARASITIC JAEGER** is a fairly common migrant along the coast and in Puget Sound. It is rare inland. At close range it can be identified by the two pointed central tail feathers extending beyond the rest of the tail. **POMARINE JAEGERS** (not illustrated) are regular migrants offshore; a few occur from time to time in the fall at the mouths of rivers and bays where they may be seen from jetties or headlands. They are heavier birds than are the other jaegers; the two central tail feathers are blunt and twisted, extending beyond the tail. The graceful and smaller **LONG-TAILED JAEGER** (not illustrated) shows two long, pointed central tail feathers extending well out from the tail. It is quite uncommon and is seldom observed from land but is usually found each fall by one or more of the offshore boat trips which have become increasingly popular with observers in the Pacific Northwest.

The large, robust **SOUTH POLAR SKUA** (not illustrated) is a rare offshore migrant which occasionally visits coastal gull flocks. It is a hawk-like sea bird, similar in plumage and actions to the darker jaegers, and shows large white patches in the wings. It harries other fish-eating birds.

The small, chunky **ALCIDS** are sea birds which nest on offshore rocks and headlands. They dive and swim underwater in pursuit of fish and to obtain animal life from underwater rocks. The small wings are better designed for underwater maneuvering than for flying; thus they fly with rapidly beating wings and with swift, direct flight. Most have distinct summer and winter plumages with the immatures being similar in appearance to winter adults. Alcids occur on fresh water only accidentally. During the winter months, these birds range well out to sea and are irregularly encountered along the ocean coast. At this time some of them can be found regularly in the waters surrounding the San Juan and Gulf Islands, and southward into Puget Sound. Alcids are gregarious and regularly occur in flocks throughout the year.

The penguin-like **COMMON MURRE** nests in great numbers on the cliff faces of offshore rocks and headlands, laying the single egg directly on a rocky ledge. For the most part they feed in the ocean well offshore, but are often seen flying back and forth over the surf. Numbers of these birds often wash up dead onto the beaches in late summer and fall; oil-soaked birds occasionally are found at other times of the year. Large flocks regularly visit the breeding rocks in winter but at this season they are more often at sea, well offshore. Many migrate into Puget Sound where they spend the winter.

The **PIGEON GUILLEMOT** is one of the more widespread and conspicuous alcids to summer along the rocky portions of the ocean coast and in Puget Sound. They seldom occur in large flocks, and can best be observed about suitable nesting rocks. This species lays its eggs in crevices in rocky cliff faces, in caves, under boulders, and in tunnels burrowed into soft clay banks. They frequently are observed in bays and harbors as well as offshore. The all-black breeding plumage and white wing patches are easily seen, as are the red legs and feet at close range. The Pigeon Guillemot in winter has white underparts and mottled dark and light upperparts. The wing patches can still be noted in the dark wings, and the legs and feet are still red. Pigeon Guillemots are rarely observed in winter along the ocean coast, but they remain quite common at that season in Puget Sound.

The mottled, sooty-brown summer plumage of the **MARBLED MURRELET** is quite unlike that of any other alcid which is found in the Pacific Northwest during the breeding season. Only recently was the first North American nest of this species discovered, high up in a fir tree in Big Basin State Park, Santa Cruz County, California. Immature Marbled Murrelets have been found on the forest floor but as yet no nest has been found in the Northwest.

The Marbled Murrelet is an uncommon and local summer resident all along the ocean coast and in Puget Sound. Birds are most often seen about the mouths of bays and rivers, and in the protected waters about headlands; in late summer they are common in the Gulf of Georgia and in northern Puget Sound. The slate-gray back of the winter plumage is set off by a white collar, a white strip on the back above the wings, and by white underparts. This species is a common winter resident in Puget Sound but is rarely observed at that season elsewhere in this region.

In plumage and size the **ANCIENT MURRELET** (not illustrated) closely resembles the Marbled Murrelet. The back is medium dark gray with no white bar above the wings. The black cap usually contrasts noticeably with the lighter back. It occurs as an uncommon migrant and winter resident in the Strait of Juan de Fuca and in parts of Puget Sound. On the ocean coast, Ancient Murrelets are widely scattered and are rather rare migrants and winter visitors.

Common Murre   3 Summer   Winter flying   Z. M. Schultz
L 14"

Pigeon Guillemot   Summer   Winter flying   Z. M. Schultz
L 10½"

Marbled Murrelet   Summer below   Winter above   L 8"
Z. M. Schultz

The tiny, mostly dark **CASSIN'S AUKLET** is a common migrant and summer resident in the offshore zone all along the Pacific Coast. The plumage is the same winter and summer. The white spot over the white eye, and the pale base of the bill are the only identifying patterns. They can be seen easily if fairly close.

They breed on many of the offshore rocky islands, utilizing crevices among the rocks or burrows several feet under the turf for their nests. On the breeding grounds they are active mostly at night, and are thus seldom seen there. They scatter far offshore in winter, but are regularly seen in Puget Sound all year. Occasionally in winter the peculiar **PARAKEET AUKLET** (not illustrated) may visit Puget Sound. It appears to be a Cassin's Auklet with white underparts, but has a heavier bill.

The fairly large **RHINOCEROS AUKLET** rarely shows any pattern in the dark breeding plumage, except for a few white plumes about the head and a large, banana-colored bill. In winter it is all dark. It is smaller than a murre. It is larger than the other alcids except for the equal-sized puffin. This species, too, is a bird of the offshore zone and is mostly nocturnal about the nesting grounds.

It deposits its single egg at the far end of a fairly long tunnel under the turf on offshore rocks and in protected headlands along the coast and in northern Puget Sound. Rhinoceros Auklets are fairly common winter residents in Puget Sound, but are seldom observed on the ocean coast.

The unique and colorful **TUFTED PUFFINS** are unmistakable in their summer plumage as they solemnly stand before their nesting burrows on offshore rocks and on turf-covered headland ledges. In flight Tufted Puffins appear as stocky black birds pushing their bills in front of them. The brilliant bill is made up of colored sheaths that are shed after the breeding season.

In winter these birds are all dark, with a rather thick, reddish bill and a light line over the eyes. They are common but rather localized summer residents, nesting in widely scattered colonies all along the ocean coast, through the Strait of Juan de Fuca and in the San Juan and Gulf Islands. They are most often observed on or about the nesting grounds. They scatter to sea in winter at which season they are seldom observed. On rare occasions a puffin is seen that has all white underparts. This would be the **HORNED PUFFIN** (not illustrated), a rare visitor from northern seas.

Cassin's Auklet

Z. M. Schultz
L 7"

Rhinoceros Auklet   Immature   Summer

Z. M. Schultz
L 11½"

Tufted Puffin   Summer   L 12½"

Z. M. Schultz

The **BAND-TAILED PIGEON,** found along the Pacific Coast and to a limited extent in the Rocky Mountains, is similar in appearance to the Rock Dove of city streets but is heavier and has a distinctive tail band and white stripe below the back of its crown. This bird builds a flimsy nest of twigs in our taller Douglas-firs, even in cities, and the young are first fed a fluid known as "pigeon milk" which is produced in the parent's crop. Spring arrival can be detected by a rapid, successive "rook-a-roo" call similar to a domestic pigeon. People often mistake the band-tail's call for an owl's hooting.

Band-tailed Pigeons prefer conifers mixed with open areas and hardwoods where they feed on salal, salmonberry, elderberry and blackberry fruits. When berries are not in season, grain and nuts are sought. Those who have bird feeders in the vicinity of Douglas-firs can attract our wild pigeons to grain and "supermarket" bird seed.

In the fall these pigeons congregate around mineral springs, which are favored hunting sites for this popular game bird. A few Band-tailed Pigeons remain here during winter but most go to California.

The **ROCK DOVE** needs no introduction to city dwellers, but many people inquire as to its origin, especially since most bird books fail to list it. This sometimes undesirable bird is common about cities. Colonies also occur outside cities where bridges, cliffs and barns create favorable nesting sites. Source of these birds was the wild European Rock Dove. These pigeons are escapees from domestic stocks of Rock

Mourning Dove L 10½"   Band-tailed Pigeon L 13½"
Z. M. Schultz

Rock Doves L 11"

Z. M. Schultz

Doves and are not native to this country. Pigeon breeders developed a number of color phases and, as a result, even the stock which has gone wild comes in various shades or combinations of white and brown along with the familiar iridescent blue-grays and greens most typical of this bird.

In cities they sometimes become serious pests when they nest on cornices of buildings and foul the area with excrement. Modern buildings are designed to discourage them.

Outside cities, Rock Doves feed on waste grain. In cities, they thrive on handouts and grain spilled at feed mills and docks.

The **MOURNING DOVE,** so called because of its mournful cooing sound, is a slimmer, longer tailed bird than either the Band-tailed Pigeon or Rock Dove. It occurs around fields and other open areas but comes into open residential areas to feed on spilled grain or at bird feeders. A few Mourning Doves remain for the winter but most move south in September. This is the most important game bird in the nation, but not locally.

Typically, Mourning Doves are seen along roadsides in late summer as small flocks or family groups "sitting in solemn and dignified rows on the fence wires," as aptly described by Gabrielson and Jewett in *Birds of Oregon.* When flushed, a whistling sound created by their wings is distinctive as opposed to the flapping sound of the Band-tailed Pigeon.

R. B. Horsfall

Western Screech-Owl L 8" W 22" (insert)
Short-eared Owl L 13" W 41"   Great Horned Owl L 20" W 55"

OWLS are mostly nocturnal birds of prey. They have keen night vision and a silent flight. They swallow food whole and later eject the bones, fur, etc. in pellets from the mouth. Fourteen species of owls occur in Oregon and Washington, but most are seldom seen.

The **WESTERN SCREECH-OWL** resides year around in parks and residential areas having ample trees. It is a small grayish or brownish owl with ear tufts, and is far more numerous than most people realize. Those who become familiar with its rapid series of bouncing whistles that descend in pitch appreciate this.

Screech-Owls feed mainly on mice. They nest in old woodpecker holes in dead trees, snags or stumps. It is possible to attract them to artificial nest boxes—particularly on the edge of wooded areas.

The **GREAT HORNED OWL** is found throughout the West from forest to desert. In Western Oregon it is particularly abundant along the edges of the Willamette Valley. This is a large-eared owl, popularly called "hoot owl" because of its "hoo, a-hoo, a-hoo" call given at night. Various hair raising screeches are also given. Hooting is heaviest in winter because nesting begins in February. An old hawk or crow nest is most often used.

Presence of a Great Horned Owl in spring or summer is commonly revealed by excited Robins which disregard their territoriality to pester and scold the disdainful owls.

Great Horned Owls feed on rats, mice, rabbits and skunks.

The similar, but smaller and slimmer, **LONG-EARED OWL** (not illustrated) is a common but seldom seen resident of thick brushy patches, mainly east of the Cascades. The long ear tufts, or horns, emerging near the center of the head, and the rusty face are distinctive.

The **SHORT-EARED OWL** is a daylight, as well as night-time, hunter of fields, prairies and marshes. This owl's flight is erratic and bouncing and the broad wing strokes are slow and relaxed. It is most common in winter, but many remain to nest in extensive dry grass meadowlands.

The **COMMON BARN-OWL** is a rather common resident that attracts attention by nesting and roosting in open barns and abandoned houses. They are most often observed in rural areas but they regularly visit city grain elevators and warehouse districts. From below many individuals appear pure white in flight. The golden-colored upperparts and "monkey face" are distinctive. They are highly valued as most efficient mousers.

107

Common Barn-Owl   *L 14" W 44"*

A.C. Fisher

Snowy Owl

Z. M. Schultz
L 20" W 55"

The large, conspicuous **SNOWY OWL** is a rare and irregular winter visitor from the far north. Its bright white plumage speckled and barred with black, and its liking for open meadow and dune lands attract immediate attention. In "flight" years they may appear anywhere in the Northwest, otherwise they are seldom observed. One or more of these great birds can be found most winters in the meadowlands about the mouth of the Fraser River south of Vancouver, British Columbia.

The **BURROWING OWL** is an uncommon but widespread bird of dry open meadows, farms and sage flats. They nest underground in abandoned squirrel or badger burrows, and are most often observed standing on a mound or clod at the entrance hole or atop a nearby fence post. Their faded brown plumage and long legs are distinctive. Often when approached a bird will bob up and down or sway from side to side emitting a series of "poop-poop-poop" calls.

Burrowing Owl   108   L 8" W 22"

Z. M. Schultz

Z. M. Schultz
Northern Pygmy-Owl   L 6" W 15"

The feisty little **NORTHERN PYGMY-OWL** is a seldom seen resident of coniferous forest edges even though it is often abroad during the day. Somewhat smaller than a Robin, it preys upon sparrows and other similar sized birds. The dark patches on the back of the head resemble eyes and are often used to intimidate predators. Its whistled "toot" call is quite similar to that of the Douglas Squirrel or Chickaree and is often wrongly identified.

The similar but strictly nocturnal **NORTHERN SAW-WHET OWL** is a rarely seen resident of forested areas, most often encountered in stream bottom deciduous groves. They migrate to the lowlands in winter, often becoming victims of speeding autos as they pass over, or hunt along the roadways. The shorter tail and lack of "eyes" on the back of the head separate this bird from the Pygmy-Owl.

Northern Saw-whet Owl   L 7" W 17"
Z. M. Schultz

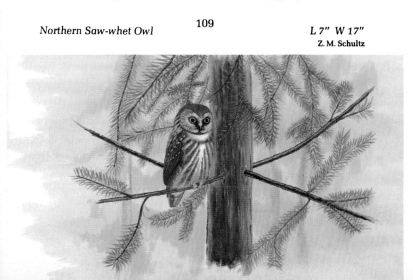

Common Nighthawk L 9″ W 23″   *Vaux's Swift L 4½″*

The **COMMON NIGHTHAWK,** popularly called "mosquito hawk" or "bullbat," is not a hawk but belongs to the same family as the Whippoorwill of the eastern and southern states, and the nightjars of Europe. By day the Nighthawk often rests on a shaded tree limb. When dusk comes, it flies in a zigzag pattern, scooping up flying insects with a wide gaping bill. Occasionally feeding occurs in daylight.

White wing, throat and tail stripes identify it from underneath, but Nighthawks are more often heard than seen because they are mostly nocturnal. While feeding, they continuously give a nasal "spee-ick" call. A loud, whirring buzz is made with wings when diving. Habitat includes cities, forests and open areas, or wherever nocturnal insects are available. Even the heart of the City of Portland has Nighthawks. They have adapted to cities by nesting on the gravelled roofs of buildings.

Nighthawks are the last summer residents to arrive, appearing about the 1st of June. They return in early fall to Mexico.

The **COMMON POORWILL** is an uncommon summer resident of dry rocky open lands mostly east of the Cascade Mountains. Being strictly nocturnal it is seldom seen but their "per-will-ip" calls are a familiar sound of calm summer evenings in many areas. Occasionally while driving country roads through rim-rock areas at night the headlights may flash on the ruby red eyes of one of these birds as it sits on the roadway. As it flutters off it might show the broad white edges on its tail. There is no white in the wings. During daylight hours Common Poorwills rest under or among rocks, or occasionally in trees.

The **VAUX'S SWIFT,** a plain, brownish swallow-like bird, can be seen dashing erratically about the sky over nearly every habitat type of this region. However, it is overlooked because it is such a high flier. It can readily be distinguished from swallows by its rapid zig-zag flight and bat-like wing beat; the wings often appear to be beating alternately but this is an illusion. Its twittery notes are also distinctive.

This is our equivalent of the eastern Chimney Swift, but rather than roosting in chimneys, Vaux's Swifts most often roost in hollow portions of old snags in forested or cut-over areas. They feed exclusively on insects obtained in flight.

Occasionally they will appear in great masses around large chimneys like the Chimney Swift. The careful observer looking over flocks of swallows in spring will often sight swifts flying above the swallows.

The noticeably larger **WHITE-THROATED SWIFT** (not illustrated) nests in colonies in niches on inaccessible cliff faces east of the Cascade Mountains. They are most often observed on warm summer evenings as they dart and swoop through deep river canyons and along cliff faces. At other times they remain high overhead out of sight. The bold black and white patterned plumage and typical swift shape and flight are distinctive. The similar sized but all dark **BLACK SWIFT** (not illustrated) is a rarely observed summer resident about Puget Sound. Both species often accompany swallows in migration.

Common Poorwill L 7"

Z. M. Schultz

The **HUMMINGBIRD** family includes our smallest birds. Their helicopter-like flight makes them unique. Under conditions of cold and stress they have the ability to go into a deep stupor in which their metabolism and temperature drop as an energy saving mechanism. Hummingbirds feed on nectar and the insects associated with nectar. They prefer red bell-shaped or tubular flowers. They seem to enjoy dive bombing larger birds.

The **RUFOUS HUMMINGBIRD** is the most common of our "hummers." It arrives in the lowlands in March with the blooming of the red-flowering currant, and later in the summer it extends its range above timberline where the alpine meadows are carpeted with flowers. The male Rufous is bright cinnamon above and below with an iridescent red throat or "gorget." The green-backed female shows much brownish at the base of the tail and along the sides of the underparts.

The **ALLEN'S HUMMINGBIRD** of coastal Southern Oregon and California is similar to the Rufous, but the male has a bright completely green back; the cinnamon coloration is restricted to the base of the tail. The female Rufous and Allen's cannot be separated at all. Some young male Rufous Hummingbirds may show greenish backs but on these birds the iridescent throat would not be complete.

♀   *Rufous Hummingbird L 3½"*   ♂

R. B. Horsfall

Anna's Hummingbird   ♂   ♀   *Z. M. Schultz*
                                                      L 3½"

The **ANNA'S HUMMINGBIRD** is a regular winter visitor to the Northwest, mostly west of the Cascade Mountains. Many remain to nest each summer. These wintering hummingbirds can become dependent upon hummingbird feeders. The Anna's is noticeably larger and much greener plumaged than the Rufous Hummingbird. The forehead of the male Anna's has the same rose iridescence as the throat. The rarer **BROAD-TAILED HUMMINGBIRD** (not illustrated), occasionally seen in summer east of the Cascades, is quite similar to the Anna's but the male has no iridescence on the forehead and, in flight, produces a loud whistling noise with its wings. The female looks like a large female Rufous Hummingbird.

Allen's Hummingbird   ♂   ♀   *L 3"*
                                                      Z. M. Schultz

The tiny **CALLIOPE HUMMINGBIRD** is a regular summer resident of the dry upland areas east of the Cascades. It may be seen anywhere in the Northwest in migration. The male's iridescent feathers are arranged in streaks on the white throat making it distinctive. The female is similar to a female Rufous but is much smaller; the wings extend well past the short tail and there is less brown in the plumage. Despite its very small size the Calliope Hummingbird is a hardy bird and is as pugnacious as any of the hummingbirds in attacking larger birds.

The **BLACK-CHINNED HUMMINGBIRD** (not illustrated) is occasionally seen in Calliope Hummingbird habitat. It is a larger bird, showing solid green upperparts and is whiter below. The male has a dull black throat showing only a trace of purple iridescence where it edges the white breast. The female shows no brownish at all.

The **HORNED LARK** is a ground dweller locally found in plowed fields and grazed grasslands. It seldom perches but sings its faint, tinkling song on the wing or from the ground. Although inconspicuous, these true larks are fairly abundant in the prairies of Western Washington, the southern Willamette Valley and the more southern valleys.

In winter they occur in restless flocks which move from place to place in short flights, uttering bell-like notes. These larks are especially conspicuous in winter in Eastern Oregon and Washington.

Horned Larks, which may represent a different race than those of the valleys, nest above timberline on our snow-capped peaks.

Horned Lark L 6½"
R. B. Horsfall

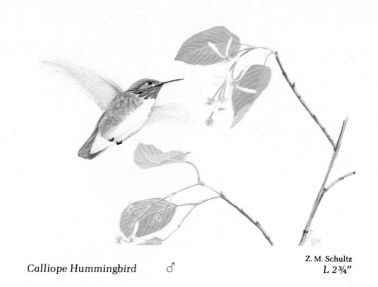

Calliope Hummingbird   ♂

The **BELTED KINGFISHER** occurs along streams, lakes and bays where it watches for small fish from a conspicuous perch or while hovering over the water. Other than the Steller's Jay, it is the only crested, blue colored bird found here. As it dives after a fish or flies along a stream, a rattling call is given.

Kingfishers take only small fish and are not a serious competitor to anglers except around fish hatcheries where they can be a real pest if ponds are not screened. Kingfishers nest in holes along stream banks and are permanent residents.

♂   ♀   Belted Kingfisher L 12"

Red-shafted
♂ *Flicker L 11"*
R. B. Horsfall

WOODPECKERS are tree surgeons in the sense that they remove dead wood to obtain food or construct nest sites. Healthy, live wood is more difficult to work and seldom has insects. A special foot structure combined with a tail which serves as a prop enables woodpeckers to perch on vertical tree trunks.

The **NORTHERN FLICKER** is our most numerous woodpecker. No other woodpecker found here resembles the flicker with its black spotted breast, black bib, and brick red coloring under the wings. Its rhythmic, dipping flight is distinctive, and unlike other woodpeckers, it hops about on the ground. Females can be separated from males by the absence of the red mustache.

The flicker described above has been known as the RED-SHAFTED FLICKER, but it readily interbreeds with the YELLOW-SHAFTED FLICKER of the East. The latter has a black mustache and red crescent on the back of the head as well as yellow under the wings. Hybrids between Yellow and Red-shafted Flickers are often seen here. Since the two Flickers freely hybridize in a large zone of overlap, both have been lumped as the Northern Flicker.

Flickers are extremely adaptable to a variety of habitats ranging from seashore to mountain to desert. They like to drum on metal surfaces and sometimes chisel holes in buildings. Despite these bad habits, they make nest holes in trees for other birds and pick ants from the ground with their sticky tongues. A large part of their diet, in fact, is ants along with berries, including those of poison oak.

Around homes, we can attract Flickers to suet. Occasionally they will accept an artificial nest box.

The "wicker-wicker-wicker" and "wake-up, wake-up" calls of the Flicker are familiar sounds.

116

The **PILEATED WOODPECKER** is anything but common in the Northwest, but because of its conspicuous nature we are including it here. This is our only Crow-sized woodpecker with a flame red crest. Mature or nearly mature coniferous forests with large dead trees and snags constitute its northwest home. Vertical excavations on dead trunks are the work of this woodpecker in search of insect larvae.

Its call is similar to a Flicker's but is much louder and provides an almost eerie feeling in a dark forest. In the West, this is a shy bird but it does get into Forest Park within the City of Portland. Pileated Woodpeckers feed on insects, ants and berries.

LEWIS' WOODPECKER is most un-woodpeckerlike with a shiny, greenish-black jacket, rosy breast, and Crow-like flight. It sometimes sallies out flycatcher style to capture flying insects. This woodpecker occurs in small loose flocks in association with oaks and cotton-woods. Distribution seems confined to isolated locations but, even in these, its occurrence is unpredictable.

Pileated Woodpecker L 15"　　　　*Lewis' Woodpecker L 9"*

R. B. Horsfall

R. B. Horsfall

Hairy Woodpecker
L 7½"

Downy Woodpecker
L 5¾"

Acorn Woodpecker
L 8"

The **HAIRY WOODPECKER,** like its smaller counterpart, the Downy Woodpecker, has gray underparts and black and white upper parts. It can be distinguished from the Downy Woodpecker by voice and its larger size. Males of both have a red patch on the back of the head whereas females do not. The Hairy Woodpecker is found in coniferous forests and seldom gets into urban areas. Its call consists of a sharp "chink" and a whinny-like rattle.

The Hairy Woodpecker will come to suet at bird feeders near homes that adjoin coniferous forests. It is a permanent resident.

The **DOWNY WOODPECKER** is our smallest woodpecker. It tends to use the deciduous rather than coniferous woods and is regularly encountered along river bottoms in cottonwoods and willows. Compared to the Hairy Woodpecker, it is a much tamer bird and comes readily to tree filled city areas. A "tap-tap-tap" heard in deciduous trees is often traced to this species.

Like other woodpeckers, insects form much of the Downy Woodpecker's diet, so suet is attractive.

Calls of the Downy Woodpecker are similar to the Hairy Woodpecker but are not as loud or harsh.

The **ACORN WOODPECKER,** often referred to as the California Woodpecker, is confined almost strictly to oak groves. Its clown-like appearance is best described by the illustration. These birds are especially common in the Rogue and Umpqua River Valleys. In recent years their range has spread into the Corvallis area and northward.

Unlike most woodpeckers, Acorn Woodpeckers are social and associate in loose colonies. They take acorns and other nuts for food. Insects are a minor part of their diet. Acorns are stored in the bark of dead wood and even in utility poles.

The **WHITE-HEADED WOODPECKER** is a distinctive but very quiet resident of the Ponderosa pine forests east of the crest of the Cascade Mountains. It is fairly common but its reserved habits make it obscure and difficult to observe. It is most often seen as it slowly works over the tree trunks searching for insect and larvae. It silently flutters from tree to tree flashing large white wing patches. Only the male shows the red nape patch.

White-headed Woodpecker   L 7¾"
Z. M. Schultz

Z. M. Schultz
Red-naped Sapsucker L 7¾"

SAPSUCKERS, unlike most other woodpeckers, penetrate live wood. Horizontal rows of holes, each about 1/4" in diameter, seen on fruit and shade trees are the work of sapsuckers. Sap oozes from the holes and is fed upon by the sapsuckers along with insects and ants attracted to the sap. Sapsuckers often cause problems about orchards. Like the Flicker, they will hammer on hollow or metal surfaces to attract a mate or defend a territory against others of their kind.

The widespread **YELLOW-BELLIED SAPSUCKER** occurs in two recognizable races or subspecies. The western race, regularly found in the Northwest east of the Cascade Crest, is called the Red-naped Sapsucker. It differs from the birds found further east by a red patch on the back of its head.

The bright **RED-BREASTED SAPSUCKER** is often confused with the Red-headed Woodpecker, a bird of Eastern North America, that does not occur here. This species is the common sapsucker west of the Cascade Mountains.

Red-breasted Sapsucker L 7¾"
R. B. Horsfall

Williamson's Sapsucker ♀ ♂

Z. M. Schultz
L 8¼"

The showy **WILLIAMSON'S SAPSUCKER** occurs as a summer resident in open coniferous forests east of the Cascade Mountains. The bright black and white male differs considerably from the brown-barred female. Both show bright yellow bellies. The Williamson's drills rows of holes on tree trunks like other sapsuckers but these workings are less often seen. This is a very active woodpecker and often becomes quite noisy.

The **BLACK-BACKED WOODPECKER** (not illustrated) is an interesting but uncommon resident of lodgepole pine and other high elevation coniferous forests. Its sedate demeanor and quiet ways make it quite difficult to locate. The sound of falling bark chips as it searches for insects is often the only indication of its presence. The solid black back and conspicuously barred flanks are distinctive. The male has a bright lemon-yellow forehead patch.

The similarly-plumaged **THREE-TOED WOODPECKER** (not illustrated) differs in having a black and white barred "ladder back." The males also show the distinctive yellow forehead. This species is seen even less often than the Black-backed and appears to prefer forests of higher elevations. Both these woodpeckers are attracted to snaggy forests and tracts of burned or dead trees. Both clear a wide patch of bark from around their nesting holes in live trees, thus making them most conspicuous to visitors in the high mountain forests.

FLYCATCHERS are sparrow-sized birds that obtain their food by darting from open perches to seize passing insects. Their alert, upright stance and restless behavior is distinctive. Many are similar in plumage and are best identified by voice and habitat preferences. Almost all leave during the winter months.

The vociferous **ASH-THROATED FLYCATCHER** is a distinctive bird of brushy deciduous woodlots in the drier more open areas of the Northwest, seldom occurring west of the Cascades north of Grants Pass. Its loud "pee-wheeur" and "prr-it" call notes attract attention to the bird hiding in the shadowy branches of a nearby tree. The bright cinnamon patches on the wings and tail are often "flashed" when perched and are quite noticeaole in flight.

Ash-throated Flycatcher
L 6½″
Z. M. Schultz

R. B. Horsfall
Western Kingbird L 7"

The **WESTERN KINGBIRD** is a bright yellow, Robin-sized flycatcher with white outer tail feathers. It is common in the dry, open areas of the Northwest, occurring only randomly in the interior valleys west of the Cascades. It is a bird of open areas with scatterings of brush or trees and farm buildings. Kingbirds are fence wire and utility pole perchers. Westerns often place their nest on or behind power transformers on the poles. They are noisy and pugnacious toward other species and will drive hawks and Crows from their neighborhood. Food is about 90 percent insects, taken in typical flycatcher style by sallies from a perch.

The **EASTERN KINGBIRD** occupies nesting territories about ponds or along streams, placing the nest in the fork of a nearby tree. It occurs in the drier sections of the Northwest, mostly east of the Cascades. Like the Western Kingbird this is a very noisy and aggressive bird, chasing off any large bird flying too near. The sharply marked black tail with the white terminal band is distinctive. Like all kingbirds, the Eastern Kingbird has a concealed red crown patch.

Eastern Kingbird   L 6¾"
Z. M. Schultz

R. B. Horsfall

Olive-sided Flycatcher L 6¼"   *Western Wood-Pewee L 5¼"*
Willow Flycatcher L 4¾"

The **OLIVE-SIDED FLYCATCHER** is conspicuous for its ringing call given from a snag-top tree within a coniferous forest. It uses the highest tops as perches and usually feeds above the forest canopy. A "pip-pip-pip" call, and another which sounds like "hic-three beers" help identify this bird. When observed from below, the dusky gray breast with a light streak down the center appears as a partially opened vest.

The **WESTERN WOOD-PEWEE** is a medium-sized flycatcher that gives a sad "pee-ar" call even on a hot day when all other birds are silent. This flycatcher is particularly common along open wood edges but it regularly is found in the shade below the canopy of open woodlands. It is a rather dark bird blending well with its chosen haunts. It is a common bird throughout the Northwest.

The term **'EMPIDONAX FLYCATCHER'** is given to a group of similar plumaged flycatcher species having olive-gray backs, light eye rings, wing bars and with light underparts often showing a yellowish cast. Each has distinctive call notes and habitat preferences that will identify them. They are almost impossible to identify in migration.

The **WILLOW FLYCATCHER,** illustrated here, is the brownest of this group. It occurs in brush, particularly along streams or damp bottoms. It readily comes to urban areas where there are good stands of brush. Distinctive call notes include "preep-deer" or "preep-a-deer."

The **WESTERN FLYCATCHER** is found under the canopy of both coniferous and deciduous forests in damp, dark sites. The breast of this flycatcher is yellow and it commonly gives a high pitched upward slurred whistled "pee-it." Its preference for damp areas restricts its presence east of the Cascades.

The **HAMMOND'S FLYCATCHER** is the Empidonax flycatcher of the great coniferous forests of the Northwest. It is an olive-gray backed bird that feeds high in the forest canopy, only occasionally dropping down to be observed. Its calls are usually the only indication of its presence; a soft "se-put," "treep," "see-lip."

The **DUSKY FLYCATCHER** is a much grayer bird than the Hammond's and occurs in more open dry brushy areas of mid to high elevations. It seldom forages in trees or brush above twenty feet in height. Its calls are similar to the Hammond's but higher and sharper.

The **GRAY FLYCATCHER** is the grayest of the Empidonax group and occurs in the driest areas of sagebrush flats and juniper woodlands. It has a distinctive two note "chee-ip" call.

The **SAY'S PHOEBE** gleans its insect fare from warm rocks, wooden buildings and other solid surfaces. They seldom rise more than a few feet above the groud and are usually encountered perched on rocks, fence posts, or weed stems. They readily utilize man-made structures, nesting in open barns and outbuildings or under bridges. Few farms east of the Cascades are without a pair of these friendly birds. The Say's Phoebe is one of the earliest spring migrants, arriving in mid-February each year; a few occur even in mid-winter. They might be seen anywhere in migration but are restricted to the dry open lands east of the Cascades during the nesting season. The dusty brown back, rusty belly and tail wagging habit distinguish this fairly common bird.

The **BLACK PHOEBE** (not illustrated) is a regular summer resident of California northward into Southwestern Oregon. It shares many of the habits of Say's Phoebe, including the distinctive tail wag. It is an entirely black bird except for its white belly.

Say's Phoebe

125

L 6¼"
Z. M. Schultz

Cliff Swallow
L 5"

Tree Swallow
L 5"

Violet-Green Swallow
L 4¾"

SWALLOWS are spring and summer residents which gather flying insects. Their graceful flight involves more gliding than flapping.

The **CLIFF SWALLOW**, often called "eave swallow" or "mud dauber," builds gourd shaped nests of mud pellets under building eaves. Sometimes up to 100 nests are plastered on a barn. Increasing numbers of Cliff Swallows are nesting under the eaves of homes— much to the consternation of residents. The nests are often taken over by house sparrows. East of the Cascade Range colonies of these birds occur under overhanging cliffs near streams and marshes.

The **VIOLET-GREEN SWALLOW** is well named because of its beautiful back color. It is confused with the Tree Swallow but, unlike the Tree Swallow, the white at the base of the tail extends almost across the back above the tail, providing a nearly white rump. From below, it is difficult to separate Violet-green from Tree Swallows except by voice.

The Violet-green Swallow is a distinctive western species which gets deeper into our cities than any other swallow. It nests in artificial boxes and in cracks in buildings where it can find spots not occupied by House Sparrows. Seemingly, there are not as many Violet-green Swallows today as 20 years ago, perhaps because of a general reduction in flying insects.

The steel blue-backed **TREE SWALLOW** is found near water and has a gurgly call. It often feeds over fields and meadows and barely penetrates cities. Old woodpecker holes, often over water, are readily taken along with artificial nest boxes by Tree Swallows. It is possible to build up high nesting densities of these swallows through use of nest boxes.

With Violet-green and Tree Swallows the first to arrive in late February or early March, they are considered harbingers of spring. In late summer swallows gather into large flocks and perch in long rows on utility wires.

The **BARN SWALLOW**, because of its long, deeply forked tail, is perhaps the most graceful of this group. Rather than nesting in colonies like Cliff Swallows, Barn Swallows' nests are usually found singly. Where Barn Swallows nested before arrival of the white man is unknown, but today they nest inside barns, sheds and garages, and on bridge beams. Their nests are open, cup-shaped mud structures filled with grass and feathers. Barn Swallows are found about farms and along the coast but do not come into our large cities.

The **PURPLE MARTIN** is almost a rarity in our region but is mentioned because so many people from eastern and southern states ask about it. Few martin nesting colonies occur in Washington or Oregon, and these are mostly confined to old woodpecker holes in snags and piling. However, several colonies are present in downtown buildings of Tacoma and Seattle. Erecting apartment-type martin houses here has, to date, been a wasted effort.

The **NORTHERN ROUGH-WINGED SWALLOW** is a brown-plumaged frequenter of stream bottoms where it builds nesting cavities in earthen banks.

L 7″   L 6″   L 4¾″
Purple Martin   *Barn Swallow*   *Northern Rough-winged Swallow*

R. B. Horsfall

Bank Swallow

Z. M. Schultz
L 4¾"

The social **BANK SWALLOW** is seldom observed away from its breeding colony. Nesting in holes dug in steep river banks, road cuts, or gravel pits, they become locally abundant where proper soils provide ideal texture to maintain the nest hole. These soils are found almost exclusively east of the Cascades and colonies of many hundreds can be found in several areas. A few individuals may join other migrant swallows and occur anywhere in the Northwest. The dark brownish back of the Bank Swallow often causes confusion with Rough-winged Swallow but the light throat and breast crossed by a distinct band will distinguish this species. Both brown-backed swallows may occur in the same nesting colony.

The **PINYON JAY** has the unique habit of remaining in a social flock throughout the year. They nest in colonies, helping each other feed and raise the young, then wander over the countryside, often in huge noisy flocks. Its grayish-blue plumage and un-jaylike habits are often confusing but its raucous Crow-like calls are distinctive. Pinyon Jays are restricted to the ponderosa pine forests on the eastern slopes of the Cascade Range and into the adjacent juniper-sage flats. They seldom wander north of the Columbia River.

Black-billed Magpie

Z. M. Schultz
L 18"

The **BLACK-BILLED MAGPIE** is a common and conspicuous bird of the open country east of the Cascade Mountains. Small numbers occasionally drift westward to visit during the non-breeding season. Its iridescent black and white plumage and long expressive tail are distinctive. Its large bulky nest is placed in brushy thickets or in trees near water and can be recognized by the stick roof built over the top of the nest, apparently to shade the young. Owls and other birds and mammals often use deserted Magpie nests as a roost or for nesting.

Magpies are efficient scavengers about ranches and along roadways. Large, raucous flocks wander over the countryside during the non-breeding season visiting feed lots and farmlands. The primary foods of this bird are insects and carrion. They occasionally pick insects from farm animals, aggravating old injuries or creating new ones. This raises the ire of many ranchers, but most realize the beneficial work of these entertaining rascals.

Pinyon Jay L 9"
Z. M. Schultz

Steller's Jay L 11"
R. B. Horsfall

The **STELLER'S JAY,** slightly larger than a Robin, crested and a showy blue and black, is the only bird in the Northwest so marked. This bird is the western equivalent of the Blue Jay so familiar to the eastern half of the continent. It has many of the characteristics of its powder-blue-and-white eastern counterpart, including a combination of both boldness and caution and a variety of noisy, raucous calls and screams. Steller's Jays imitate hawk calls. Unknown to most people, these jays have a seldom used soft, sweet song.

This jay is frequently cited by biologists as the bird symbol of the coniferous forests of the West. It ranges from sea level to timberline, but also comes readily into farm and city yards if an abundance of trees is present for cover. Its appetite for suet, hotcakes or nuts seems boundless. Steller's Jays sneak about as if they have a guilt complex and quickly move away when man emerges from his door. They have a bad reputation among walnut and filbert growers.

Steller's Jays also feed on carrion, eggs and young of small birds, and seeds. When they have gorged on all the suet in a bird feeder, they will accept commercial wild bird seed. Despite their unpopular food habits, our forests would seem empty without their beauty and calls.

These birds are nonmigratory, and single individuals often live many years.

The **BLUE JAY** is a common bird of the Eastern United States that rarely occurs in the Northwest. Steller's and Scrub Jays are often called Blue Jays, a practice that is erroneous and misleading.

Z. M. Schultz

Blue Jay   L 10"

The **SCRUB JAY,** unlike the previous species, does not have a crest
and is a bright blue rather than a blackish blue. Its long tail is also a
distinctive characteristic. This species has been extending its range
steadily northward, and today we see Scrub Jays in Southwestern
Washington. Perhaps it is appropriate that this bird was formerly
called the California Jay since it is typically a more southern species
of dry, brushy oak slopes. Scrub Jays, however, are coming into cities
more and more. They occur both as individuals and pairs and are
bold, wary or crafty, depending upon the situation.

They frequent bird feeders where they gobble down suet and
chase other birds away. In fact, their raucous calls alone make many
small birds scatter for cover. Food includes small birds, eggs, acorns,
nuts, grain, berries and insects.

131

Scrub Jay L 10"
Z. M. Schultz

Gray Jay L 10″ above
Clark's Nutcracker L 11″

Common Crow L 17″

The **GRAY JAY** is a mountain bird but sometimes occurs at 2,000 feet elevation or lower in foothills of the Coast and Cascade Ranges.

This bird is one of the few which inhabit mature mountain forests where it is familiar the year around to campers and loggers as "camp robber." A Gray Jay will silently glide from a secluded perch in a fir or hemlock to rob food from a picnicker's table or follow hikers or cross-country skiers for a share of lunch. With coaxing, they will take food out of a person's hand.

These birds are not always silent. In fact, they have a variety of noisy calls and whistles. Typically, they occur in loose flocks or family groups.

Various races of Gray Jays have been called Oregon Jay and Canada Jay.

The **CLARK'S NUTCRACKER** or Clark's Crow resembles the Gray Jay but is larger and inhabits sparsely timbered areas at timberline or where rocky outcroppings occur in the high mountains. It makes long, Crow-like flights over the tree tops as opposed to the tree-to-tree glides of the Gray Jay. The raucous grating calls of the Nutcracker are distinctive. This bird is also referred to as "camp robber."

The **COMMON CROW** hardly requires an introduction because it is a universally known species that concentrates about cities, agricultural areas and lowlands along rivers. It gives the distinctive and well known "caw-caw-caw" call.

Crows usually nest in deciduous trees along streams but wander about in the fall and winter in loose flocks. During this period they congregate at night in roosts with much noise and commotion. The same roost sites are used night after night and serve many square miles.

Crows feed on a variety of foods including insects, nuts, fruit, carrion, birds' eggs and nestlings.

Coastal Crows are noticeably smaller than those from the interior and often give slightly different calls. Populations along the Washington coast and about Puget Sound have been separated as a distinct species, the **NORTHWESTERN CROW** (not illustrated), but this distinction is not universally accepted.

The **COMMON RAVEN** replaces the Crow in unsettled, wild areas. It is most abundant in the open rangelands east of the Cascades and in the rugged mountain ranges. It regularly visits coastal areas during the non-breeding season, and a few pair remain to nest in the wilder sections. Ravens do not particularly like cultivated or settled areas but visit them occasionally. Ravens differ from Crows by being considerably larger, having a more massive bill, and showing a long wedged tail. The Raven's croaking calls are distinctive. Ravens often fly and soar like a hawk. Like Crows, they gather in large nightly roosts during the non-breeding season.

Common Raven   *L 21"*
Z. M. Schultz

R. B. Horsfall

Black-capped
Chickadee L 4½"

Chestnut-backed
Chickadee L 4¼"

The friendly **CHICKADEES** are permanent residents within their ranges, often becoming tame. A troop of chickadees clinging like tiny acrobats to branch tips as they inspect for insect eggs or larvae is a familiar sight in the winter woods. During this period they often join flocks of kinglets, nuthatches and Creepers. Although each chickadee species prefers a different habitat, they may flock together and visit the same feeding stations. All chickadees nest in holes in trees but will readily accept artificial nest boxes set out for them.

Chickadees eat seeds and insects, and at the bird feeder take sunflower seeds, peanuts and suet.

The **BLACK-CAPPED CHICKADEE** is readily distinguished from other chickadees by its gray coat and deep black and white head pattern. Black-caps prefer broad-leafed trees like cottonwoods, willows and imported shade trees. They have a distinctive "chick-a-dee-dee" call and several whistling call notes given in spring.

The **CHESTNUT-BACKED CHICKADEE** prefers dark, humid coniferous forests but comes into urban areas having Douglas-firs. The call of this chickadee is hardly recognizable as a chickadee. It is nasal compared to the clear call of the Black-capped. Chestnut-backed Chickadees often remain high in the tree-tops but can be attracted to lower levels with imitated bird calls. The bright reddish plumage is distinctive.

The **MOUNTAIN CHICKADEE** looks much like the Black-capped Chickadee but is grayer and shows a distinctive white line over the eye. It is a bird of drier more open coniferous forests. It is the chickadee most often seen east of the Cascade Mountain Crest. Mountain Chickadees occasionally visit western lowlands during the winter months.

The **BOREAL CHICKADEE** (not illustrated) is a resident of the high mountain forests of Canada and Northeastern Washington. It is quite similar to the Black-capped Chickadee but is a dark brownish-gray bird showing black only on the bib. Brownish young of other chickadees are often mistaken for this bird. Boreal Chickadees rarely stray from the high mountains.

Mountain Chickadee   L 4¼"
                                                    A.C. Fisher

Plain Titmouse L 5"
Z. M. Schultz

The **PLAIN TITMOUSE** is a gray, crested chickadee-like bird found in Southern Oregon valleys, particularly where oaks occur. It has chickadee-like habits but is not as sociable. It is attracted to bird feeders and artificial nest boxes much like chickadees.

The **BROWN CREEPER** spirals up tree trunks in seach of insects and flies downward to the next tree, to spiral upward again. It is found in all forested areas and is far more common than generally realized. Because it feeds on bark insects, it has a year-round food supply and often keeps company with flocks of kinglets and chickadees.

The Creeper's high call note is similar to a Golden-crowned Kinglet. A seldom heard beautiful clear song of five whistled notes is distinctive.

Creepers nest behind slabs of bark, and people can attract nesters by nailing slabs of bark loosely againt tree trunks so a crevice is formed.

Brown Creeper L 4¾"
R. B. Horsfall

The **BUSHTIT**, next to the hummingbird, is our smallest bird. Were it not for its long tail, it would appear even smaller. Most of the year bushtits occur in constantly moving loose flocks that wander in a follow-the-leader fashion. They communicate in high-pitched twittering notes which hold the flock together.

In spring the flocks break up temporarily. A mated pair builds a hanging nest of lichens and moss which resembles a dirty old boot sock hung from a limb. The nest, with a minute hole for an entrance, may be as long as 21 inches.

Bushtits come to bird feeders intermittently for suet but do not remain long. Their food is over 80 percent insects.

The **WRENTIT,** found only in Oregon, California and Baja California, is a secretive resident of brushy hillsides and the coastal strip. In Oregon it reaches greatest abundance on the coast in the salal and manzanita thickets. It also extends into the Coast Range and the Rogue River and Umpqua River valleys. The Columbia River appears to be a barrier to its spread into Washington. A sharp ringing song of two or three staccato notes followed by about six notes that run together and slide downward are the best evidence of the Wrentit's presence for it is seldom seen in the open.

Bushtit L 3½"
(left)
Wrentit L 5¼"
(right)
R. B. Horsfall

American Dipper L 5¾"

The **AMERICAN DIPPER** or Water Ouzel is a year-round resident of rocky, rushing mountain streams. It enters our valleys where there are dashing torrents.

Typically we envision a Dipper as teetering up and down on a rock protruding above the water. Its gray color blends with the rock. If it were not for teetering motion, busy forays after aquatic insects and a staccato call, it would go unnoticed.

Dippers sometimes forage completely submerged in rushing streams by walking on the streambed. Even the nest is part of the aquatic environment—a damp, mossy structure usually placed behind a waterfall.

Their liquid song is a treat to hear, especially in the gloom of winter. The Dipper is a companion to the Steelhead fisherman and brightens the somber winter day with a flood of brilliant notes that rise from the noise of rushing water.

NUTHATCHES are small white and bluish-gray birds that go head first down tree trunks or hang from the undersides of limbs. The **RED-BREASTED NUTHATCH** has a white line over its eye and is common in conifers. It spends more time gleaning through branches than the slightly larger **WHITE-BREASTED NUTHATCH** which prefers working over tree trunks, especially those of oaks or cottonwoods. Seldom are more than one or two nuthatches seen at a time, but they enjoy company of chickadees, Creepers and kinglets.

Nuthatch calls are similar, but a nasal "yank-yank-yank" coming from a stand of conifers is sure to be a Red-breasted Nuthatch. The White-breasted Nuthatch more often gives single calls including a descending "keer."

R. B. Horsfall

R. B. Horsfall

Red-breasted Nuthatch
L 4"

White-breasted Nuthatch
L 5"

The **PYGMY NUTHATCH** is a common resident of the Ponderosa pine forests east of the Cascade Crest. Its plain bluish-gray back, brownish head and quiet habits render it inconspicuous. Its soft, twittery voice is distinctive but is often overlooked. It is a friendly bird and is often found in campgrounds and picnic areas working low near the base of the trees.

Nuthatches eat insects, nuts and seeds and come readily for suet, nutmeats and sunflower seeds at bird feeders.

Pygmy Nuthatch L 3½"
Z. M. Schultz

139

Winter
Wren L 3¼"
R. B. Horsfall

WRENS can all be described as highly energetic small, brown birds that feed almost entirely on insects.

The **WINTER WREN,** one of our smallest birds, has a gurgling, clear flowing song with amazing volume that comes from the deepest, darkest corners of the forest. A distinctive scolding "chick-chick" call demonstrates their abundance in second growth timber with a brushy understory when they move into valleys for the winter.

The **BEWICK'S WREN** is one of the commonest of birds in brushy cut-over areas and reaches many undeveloped portions of our cities, and even into gardens. It has a distinctive white line over its eye and is larger than the Winter and House Wren. It begins singing in February and has a loud buzz for a call.

Bewick's Wren L 4½"   House Wren L 4¼"
R. B. Horsfall

The **HOUSE WREN,** like the Winter Wren, lacks distinctive markings but instead of dwelling near the forest floor, it frequents open tree stands. It occurs here as a very scattered summer resident in both city and country but favors old orchards and forest edges, especially where old trees and rundown buildings provide an abundance of nest cavities.

The males often disperse in attempts to attract females to new areas by singing and nest building. Sticks are placed in cavities or artificial nest boxes, but more often than not, their efforts fail to attract females and the nests are abandoned. House Wrens are aggressive toward other birds despite their minute size, Nest boxes with entrance holes 7/8″ in diameter will admit them to the exclusion of other birds.

House Wrens sing throughout the day.

The effervescent **MARSH WREN** is a conspicuous resident of marshes and roadside ditches. Its small size, brownish plumage and secretive ways would keep it well hidden but for its persistent habit of scolding an intruder with a tirade of sputtery calls and trills, usually given as the bird darts about just out of sight. Occasionally one will mount a tall stem showing the white streakings on its back and bobbing its tiny tail in unison with its scoldings.

In spring the male will build numerous nests about the marsh in hopes a female will select one for her home; the rest remain empty. Many Marsh Wrens remain to winter but most migrate to more hospitable climates returning in early spring.

Marsh Wren L 4″

Z. M. Schultz

The pale **ROCK WREN** blends well with shale and rock outcroppings found in the drier areas of the Northwest. Rather rare and uncommon in the more humid western sections, it finds the sun baked deserts east of the Cascades more to its liking. Like all wrens it would be difficult to observe but for its loud and persistent scolding that draws attention to it as it scurrys about the rocky ledges. Most Rock Wrens winter far to the south but a few remain in the more protected areas.

The **CANYON WREN** is also a lover of the desert country and is seldom found in the humid western areas. Unlike the Rock Wren, the Canyon Wren seeks out darker, cooler outcroppings sheltered from the scorching sun. They are often found along the streams and rivers where high, steep rimrocks provide ideal habitat. In keeping with its chosen haunts Canyon Wrens are dark plumaged but for a conspicuous white breast that can be seen for some distance. Its beautiful song is a descending series of loud, clear double notes.

Canyon Wren   L 4½″
                                                        Z. M. Schultz

Rock Wren

Z. M. Schultz
L 4¾"

The **SAGE THRASHER** is a slim Robin-like summer resident of the dry sage-brush deserts east of the Cascade Mountains. Its loud, long beautiful song, heard in early summer, gives indication of the abundance of this rather secretive bird. Its brownish plumage, spotted underparts and Robin-like shape is distinctive.

The **GRAY CATBIRD** (not illustrated) is similar to the Sage Thrasher in size, shape, song and actions but its plain dark gray plumage and rusty undertail patch is quite different. It occurs in thick brushy streamside areas from Northeast Oregon northward.

Sage Thrasher   *L 7"*
Z. M. Schultz

Varied Thrush L 8"

R. B. Horsfall
America Robin L 8½"

The **AMERICAN ROBIN** comes closest to being an all-American bird—it is both loved and cursed. It is equally at home in cities, farms and open forests. In the northeastern and North-central States, the robin is a harbinger of spring, but in the Northwest these birds occur year-round. However, they aren't necessarily the same Robins. The Robin pair that sets up a territory in your backyard in March and departs in September or October is replaced by other Robins which come and go throughout the winter in flocks. These birds represent migrants from the mountains or northern lands. Robins nest northward as far as there are trees and as high as timberline, but cannot live in such areas in winter.

Robins catching earthworms are a source of amusement. However, in blueberries, strawberries, or a cherry tree even one robin can turn from friend to foe in the eyes of some humans. We can be a foe to the robin, too. During spring and summer, Robins require a high protein diet for egg production and feeding their young. People who apply certain pesticides to their lawn to kill earthworms, and thereby deprive moles of their food supply, are likewise destroying the Robin's source of food.

During nesting season Robins are highly territorial. Each pair defends against all other Robins an area having food, nesting cover, singing perches, and other essentials for reproduction. This leaves room for only a given number of Robins to nest, and serves to keep the population in check with the food supply. However, Robins are extremely prolific, with each successful pair producing about two broods of four each, annually. Various population control mechanisms keep us from being overrun with Robins.

Without mortality, we would have in ten years 19,500,000 robins resulting from one pair. The family cat plays a role here, especially when the young are just out of the nest and unable to fly. Nature intends for low survival rate among young songbirds.

In winter Robins often appear in immense flocks, and at dusk the flocks gather to roost by tens or even hundreds of thousands of birds. Holly orchards are favorite roost sites. From the roosts, Robins range out over wide areas to feed. Favorite winter foods include fruits or berries such as apples, European mountain ash, cotoneaster and holly. Some years the flocks are in hundreds rather than thousands. This does not necessarily indicate an overall decline in Robins. Wintering and migrating birds are highly mobile and live opportunistically in accordance with food supplies. It is reasonable to suspect, for example, that more Robins might winter west of the Cascades when the juniper (*Juniperus occidentalis*) berry crop east of the Cascades is poor.

Man probably increased Robin populations in America over what occurred formerly because fields, lawns and irrigated areas make much better Robin habitat than mature forests.

The **VARIED THRUSH,** popularly called "Alaska Robin," is a striking Robin-like bird with a black breast band. It raises numerous questions concerning its identity when it appears in northwest cities in winter, often with flocks of Robins. The females are not so brightly colored as the male shown.

Locally appearing Varied Thrushes come from nearby mountains and probably Canada and Alaska. Some winters even the coast receives an invasion of these thrushes.

Breeding habitats are dark, damp forests. In winter old orchards and stands of trees, brush and grasses are favorite sites, but the birds also occur in urban areas.

Even in winter these thrushes give their single shrill, whistled notes on various high pitches. Each note is about one second duration with a longer pause between. Singing reaches a peak in May and June in the darkest forests of the Cascade and Coast Ranges. They particularly like to sing in gloomy weather. Call is a single "twerp."

Food consists of worms, snails, insects and other animal life along with seeds and fruit. They forage mostly on the ground and are fond of fallen apples. It is often possible to attract them to bird feeders with fruit or seeds.

R. B. Horsfall

Hermit Thrush L 6"   Swainson's Thrush L 6¼"

The **HERMIT THRUSH** and **SWAINSON'S THRUSH** are birds of the shadows and heavy foliage and are conspicuous only to those who recognize their songs and calls. Those who live around large patches of mixed evergreens and deciduous brush and trees often have Swainson's Thrushes from May to October. Swainson's Thrushes go to Central America for the winter, but a few Hermit Thrushes winter locally in lowlands.

Both of these birds are outstanding songsters, but only in their nesting habitat from May into July do they sing their full song. The song of the Swainson's Thrush, usually given at dawn and dusk, is a series of upward spiraling phrases described as "cordelia, cordelia, cordelia." Also conspicuous are two clear whistled calls, one an upward rising slurred note and the other with little pitch change.

In the West one must go to the high mountains to hear the flute-like song of the Hermit Thrush, but in winter it utters an unmusical "twerp" or "twerp-twerp" which helps distinguish it from the Fox Sparrow.

Both of these thrushes feed on insects and wild fruits. They often crash into windows. The Hermit Thrush has a reddish-brown tail as contrasted to the distinct brown one of the Swainson's. Our local subspecies of the Swainson's Thrush was formerly called Russet-backed Thrush.

Mountain Bluebird   *L 6"*

BLUEBIRDS are conspicuous lovers of the open areas, nesting in holes in trees and fence posts, and feeding on insects garnered from, or near, the ground. When available, they will eat fruits and berries. They are friendly and confiding birds and will readily come to artificial nesting boxes set out for them.

The iridescent sky-blue plumage of the **MOUNTAIN BLUEBIRD,** showing no rusty coloration, is distinctive. It is a summer resident of the drier sections of the Northwest, seldom visiting the humid western areas except in transit. Great flocks often gather in migration; a few remain in winter.

WESTERN BLUEBIRDS are permanent residents in low to moderate elevations throughout the Northwest, gathering in flocks to wander in search of food during the winter months. The deep blue back, rusty breast and hunched up appearance is distinctive. This friendly bird has disappeared from many areas due primarily to the loss of proper nesting habitat. The placing of nest boxes about farm fields and meadows has allowed them to remain common in these sections, although swallows, Starlings and House Sparrows compete with them for these nesting sites.

147

Western Bluebird
L 5½"
♂ *(left) and* ♀

Townsend's Solitaire

A. C. Fisher
L 6¾"

The subdued **TOWNSEND'S SOLITAIRE** is a secretive summer resident of Northwest forests, seldom observed although its loud pleasing song is often heard in the early morning hours. Small numbers visit the western lowlands in winter but most are attracted to the open woodlands east of the Cascades where Juniper berries and other fruits are available. This slim grayish-brown bird is best distinguished by the buffy wing patches, white eyering and trusting look.

WATER PIPITS nest high on the tallest mountains above tree-line, coming down to winter in lowland fields and meadows. Flocks are often encountered in migration on coastal tidal flats. Water Pipits appear as slender sparrow-like birds that walk instead of hop and regularly bob and wag their long expressive tails. The distinctive "pipit" call notes can be heard as they flit about overhead.

Water Pipit L 5½"

148

A. C. Fisher

KINGLETS are minute, flighty, olive-gray birds which, except for the female **RUBY-CROWNED KINGLET,** have bright colored patches on their crowns. The male "Ruby-crowned" can erect his fiery red crown patch, but usually it is depressed and inconspicuous. Without the crown patch showing, the Ruby-crowned Kinglet can be confused with the Huttons' Vireo.

Ruby-crowned Kinglets do not occur in summer in our lowlands, but appear in winter and especially in spring. They come as single birds or in twos, threes, or fours, and sing a sweet, musical song which gradually rises in pitch until it exceeds the high range of human hearing. "Ruby-crowns" like cities if small trees and shrubs are present.

GOLDEN-CROWNED KINGLETS, while present year-round, are most often seen in winter in mixed flocks of chickades, Creepers and nuthatches. They spend most of their time obscured in the highest foliage of conifers. A fluttering action from the ends of the lowest fir and spruce boughs draws attention to kinglets. They are also viewed when working through willows along river bottoms, and are quite tame. Their short, high-pitched squeaking or staccato "zee-zee-zee" call notes can be confused only with the Creeper. "Golden-crowns" sing from tree heights with a weak series of high-pitched notes which may first rise slightly in pitch but end with a descending run of notes.

Kinglets feed almost entirely on insects.

Ruby-crowned Kinglet
L 3¾" ♀ and ♂

Golden-crowned Kinglet
L 3½" ♂ and ♀

R. B. Horsfall

R. B. Horsfall
Cedar Waxwing L 5¾"

The **CEDAR WAXWING** is identified by its crest and soft delicate brownish plumage with red, waxlike wing spots resembling ornaments. The bright yellow tail tips can be seen even as the bird flies over. Favored habitats are brushlands mixed with small farms and second growth timber. They regularly come into cities to feed on the berries of ornamental shrubs and trees and to visit bird baths for water. After the nesting season they appear unexpectedly in restless flocks which move about in search of food, which consists of insects and both tame and wild fruits. Occasionally they dart after flying insects from a perch, flycatcher style.

Their voice is a series of high-pitched soft squeals, nearly always given in flight.

The larger, grayer **BOHEMIAN WAXWING** has a white patch in each wing, but is otherwise quite similar to the Cedar Waxwing and is often found with them. Large flocks of Bohemian Waxwings visit areas east of the Cascade Mountains in winter; a few individuals occasionally stray to westside lowlands.

Bohemian Waxwing

L 6¼"

Z. M. Schultz

Loggerhead Shrike L 7"

SHRIKES are predatory birds obtaining insects, small birds and rodents for food. They are heavy-headed birds with strong hooked bills. They hold their bodies horizontally when perched and have a low undulating flight with short periods of rapid wingbeats. They are Robin-sized birds with distinctive gray and white plumages. They often mimic songs and calls of other birds.

The **LOGGERHEAD SHRIKE** is a summer resident east of the Cascades, a few stray to the westside lowlands in migration and some may winter. It has a darker back than the Northern Shrike and the facial mask is more conspicuous and complete over the bill.

The **NORTHERN SHRIKE** nests far to the north and regularly winters throughout the Northwest in small numbers. It is a larger bird than the Loggerhead. The facial mask is confined mostly behind the eye. The lower bill often shows a light base.

Northern Shrike L 8"

151

VIREOS are small greenish-gray foliage inhabitants having rather heavy hooked bills although they feed almost entirely on insects. They are difficult to observe but their songs are distinctive.

The **SOLITARY VIREO,** formerly called Cassin's Vireo here, is a summer resident of the shrub layer of open coniferous forests. A series of upward and downward slurred notes help identify it along with wing bars and a white eye ring.

The **WARBLING VIREO,** as its name denotes, has a warbling song and is found here in summer wherever alders occur. It occurs to some extent in other deciduous trees as well, and in pre-World War II days, was seen regularly in shade trees of Portland.

The **HUTTON'S VIREO** is an uncommon year-round resident west of the Cascade Mountains. It resembles a large female Ruby-crowned Kinglet but lacks the kinglet's nervous movements and has a heavy vireo bill. Look for this bird in dense thickets and moist woodlots.

Warbling Vireo L 4¾"   *Solitary Vireo L 4¾"*

R. B. Horsfall

Z. M. Schultz
L 5″

Red-eye Vireo

RED-EYED VIREOS occur regularly in many forested areas primarily east of the Cascades. They are usually found foraging in the tops of streamside deciduous trees. Its song is a series of Robin-like "question and answer" phrases. When seen they are best identified by the gray crown and white eyeline bordered with black.

Hutton's Vireo

L 4″
Z. M. Schultz

Nashville Warbler

L 4"

WARBLERS are brightly-colored active little birds that flit through the trees and underbrush in constant search for insects. This is a large family with many different species scattered over North and South America. Many species occasionally visit the Northwest but only ten are regularly observed. Each species is distinctively plumaged but it is often difficult to observe these busy birds; they are then identified by their song. Each species prefers certain types of cover for their activities but in migration they may show up anywhere. When their insect food supply is dormant in winter most go to Mexico and South America.

The **ORANGE-CROWNED WARBLER** is a summer resident of open brushy areas. It is one of the first warblers to return in spring and during March and April is the one most likely to be seen and heard. The song, a high, weak trill, dropping off in pitch near the end, can be heard regularly in spring but the birds soon become silent and inconspicuous.

The gray-headed **MacGILLIVRAY'S WARBLER** occurs in heavy brushy areas. Low-growing alders and willows near moisture and heavily overgrown cut-over forested lands are favored sites. The five note song drops in pitch on the last two notes.

The yellow-throated **NASHVILLE WARBLER** occurs in areas similar to the MacGillivray's Warbler but are usually found in drier more exposed vegetation. Its two-part song consists of several sharp notes followed by a loud trill.

R. B. Horsfall

MacGillivray's Warbler L 4½" *Black-throated Gray*
♂ and ♀ (below) *Warbler ♂ L 4"*
Orange-crowned Warbler L 4¼"

The **BLACK-THROATED GRAY WARBLER** is a summer resident of lowland coniferous forests. It is particularly attracted to second growth Douglas-fir and regularly occurs in the juniper woodlots east of the Cascades. Its song is recognized by distinct "zee" notes rendered in a rather buzzy fashion.

HERMIT WARBLERS are summer residents of mid-elevation coniferous forests west of the Cascade Crest. They are irregular and uncommon north of the Columbia River and east of the Cascades. They most often occur in mature hemlock and Douglas-fir crowns where it is almost impossible to see them. The bright, somewhat wheezy song is similar to the Black-throated Gray Warbler but does not contain so distinctive a "zee" quality.

The hardy **TOWNSEND'S WARBLER** is a fairly common resident of the coniferous forests at high elevations, mostly above the range of the Hermit Warbler, east and west of the Cascades. A few remain to winter in the lowlands. Large flocks are often encountered passing through coastal forests in February and March, the main spring migration, however, occurs in late April. Its song is similar to the Hermit and Black-throated Gray Warblers but is less spirited than the Hermit and contains a few buzzy "zee" notes.

ermit Warbler L 4¼" ♂ and ♀
wnsend's Warbler L 4¼" ♂ (below)

R. B. Horsfall

Yellow-breasted Chat L 6¼"
Yellow-rumped Warbler L 4¾
♂ *above* ♀ *right*
R. B. Horsfall

The **YELLOW-RUMPED WARBLER** is the most widely distributed and conspicuous of Northwest warblers, except during the breeding season when they retire to the tree-tops of the coniferous forests. It is an abundant migrant and regular winter visitor to lowland woodlots and forests throughout the Northwest. Its rather plain brownish plumage is broken by yellow on the rump and on each side of the body. The male in spring assumes a beautiful and striking gray streaked plumage accented by bright yellow patches on the head, throat, rump and sides of the breast. The Yellow-rumped Warbler of eastern North America has a clean white throat in place of bright yellow; numbers regularly migrate through the Northwest and may be observed among their yellow-throated relatives.

The song of the Yellow-rumped Warbler is two parted either rising or falling in pitch. The second part is given rapidly but not trilled. The "tchip" call note is distinctive once it is learned.

The golden yellow **WILSON'S WARBLER** sports a shiny black cap on top of its head, brightest in the male and missing entirely in young birds. It is one of the commonest summer warblers in the Northwest, especially west of the Cascades. It is a bird of dense brush and small trees along forest streams and moist thickets. The heavy brushy growth in coastal coniferous forests are particularly favored. Its song is a series of loud sharp "chips" given in a chattering manner.

The bright **YELLOW WARBLER** is a summer resident of tall shade trees, streamside deciduous groves and thick shrubs. It is attracted to residential plantings and is often quite common along city streets and about farm houses. It is susceptible to many of the insecticide sprays and many areas where they are used are now without these cheery birds. Yellow Warblers appear to be all yellow, the male very bright with fine red streakings on the breast. The female and young birds are more subdued. The bright clear song of the Yellow Warbler is a rapidly delivered series of "see" notes.

Wilson's Warbler ♂ L 4¼"   Yellow Warbler ♂ L 4"
Common Yellow-throat   L 4¼" ♂

The large **YELLOW-BREASTED CHAT** is a sparrow-sized summer inhabitant of dense deciduous brush along streams and in moist meadows. It rarely allows a view of its bright throat and clean white "spectacles," but occasionally it gets carried away and mounts a tall spire above the bush-tops to observe the intruder. Despite its secretive ways, it is one of the noisiest, most enjoyable birds in its territory. Its call notes and magnificent "song" are often compared to a Mockingbird or Catbird. The intruder is often overwhelmed with a series of "hoots," "kooks," "coits," loud police whistles and various other loud noises usually given in phrases. It often can be heard on quiet summer nights voicing these same notes but in a much calmer, less excited manner.

The **COMMON YELLOWTHROAT** is a common summer resident of heavy vegetation in and about marshes, bogs and wet meadows. Marsh Wrens, rails, and blackbirds are often found nearby. Its distinctive "whitchity-whitchity-whitchity" song is a regular summer sound about its chosen haunts. In many of its actions it resembles a wren more than a warbler. The female and immature are brownish-yellow showing a clear yellow throat and buffy-yellow breast. Few other warblers occur in the marsh vegetation so loved by the Yellowthroat.

The **EUROPEAN STARLING** and **HOUSE SPARROW** are both pests and came to this country from Europe at the hand of man. The Starling is not a blackbird; it has a dumpier body and a shorter tail. It reached this area in the 1950s after spreading slowly across the continent from transplants to New York in the 1890s. The disbanded Portland Songbird Club introduced Starlings to Portland in 1889 or 1892, but that transplant was not sucessful.

Most of our wintering Starlings appear to be migrants from British Columbia and Alberta. Fortunately, they are not as abundant in summer as in winter when they are perhaps the most abundant bird in our lowlands. Immense wintering flocks feed on insects in fields. At dusk flocks fly to huge roosts in holly orchards or other dense groves of trees. The resultant excrement and stench make the Starling particularly obnoxious to man. The Starling is also a problem around bird feeders because a flock will drive away native birds while consuming suet and other foods at an unbelievable rate.

Cornices on buildings and woodpecker holes are used for nesting. The long range effect of the Starling taking woodpecker holes from native birds is not known but could be serious. Starlings cannot enter nest box holes that are less than 1½" in diameter. There is no known practical way to control Starlings which have an enormous reproductive capacity since they produce more than one brood annually and will nest colonially rather than on a territorial basis. Hopefully, their numbers will decline, as is usually the case with a new immigrant or introduction.

158

European Starling L 6"
juvenile   summer adult   winter adult

Z. M. Schultz

House Sparrow L 5¼" ♀   (left) and   ♂

Z. M. Schultz

There are some beneficial aspects because the Starling feeds largely on insects, but they also take seeds and fruit. Their song consists of numerous wheezy whistles, chirps, squeaks and rattles which often mimic native species.

The House or English Sparrow is not a true sparrow or a finch but belongs to the weaver finch family so prominent in Africa. It is unfortunate that many desirable native species are lumped with this immigrant under the term "sparrow." Some native species even look like a female House Sparrow, especially the immature Golden-crowned Sparrow.

The House Sparrow was introduced in the early 1850s to New York from England, thus giving rise to the name English Sparrow. Many importations followed, including some to other parts of the country. By 1889 or earlier, this bird was in Portland, and it reached Seattle in 1897.

House Sparrows seldom occur outside environments occupied by man. They are aggressive toward native birds, especially about bird feeders and nest boxes. It is the House Sparrow along with the Starling which keeps Violet-green Swallows from nesting in many parts of our cities. If nest boxes are not present, they nest in holes in buildings or in dense shrubbery. Two or more broods are raised per year. If nests are destroyed, House Sparrows are not discouraged; they rarely give up.

Food consists of insects, seed, and refuse. For those who have bird feeders, take note that House Sparrows can't crack sunflower seeds and don't take suet or nut meats.

Z. M. Schultz

Red-winged Blackbird L 7¼"

adult ♀   1st year ♂   adult ♂

The male **RED-WINGED BLACKBIRD** with its black plumage and gaudy red and yellow epaulets cannot be confused with any other bird of this area except the **TRICOLORED BLACKBIRD** of Southern Oregon which has a white rather than yellow bar under the red. Red-winged Blackbirds are migratory, but some remain here year-round. In winter they occur in flocks. Males arrive at nesting areas as early as February to set up territories which they stake out by singing "oak-a-leo." Females arrive later and remain inconspicuous because they are a drab brown and don't defend a territory from a singing perch. "Red-wings" are one of our commonest birds and nest wherever there are damp areas including marshes and roadside ditches. They are polygamous.

Food is mostly vegetable including corn, grain, fruit and weed seeds, but nestlings are fed insects.

The **BREWER'S BLACKBIRD** is a dry land species compared to the "Red-wing." The male in spring is iridescent black and has an ivory colored eye. Winter plumage of the male is more like the duller female. This blackbird has a distinctive gait because it walks with jerks of the head. It is found in open areas, especially agricultural lands and golf courses, and comes into cities in localized areas. Brewer's Blackbirds occur with Red-winged Blackbirds and Starlings in winter. Both blackbirds have adapted to modern agriculture, and sometimes occur in swarmlike fashion over croplands. Brewer's Blackbirds commonly use utility wires and fences for perching. Food is similar to the Red-winged Blackbird.

The **BROWN-HEADED COWBIRD** resembles a Brewer's Blackbird, but notice in spring the brownish head of the male, smaller size, and lack of a yellow eye. Immature birds are plain gray. Cowbirds invaded this area following World War II and are now abundant in spring and summer. The invasion was natural in that man did not introduce them. Perhaps it was an artificial situation in that man created good Cowbird habitat with his agriculture. Cowbirds frequent forest edges, agricultural lands and urban areas where they parasitize desirable birds like the Song Sparrow. If one sees a Song Sparrow feeding a youngster larger than itself, it is a Cowbird. Cowbirds lay their eggs in the nests of other species, and Cowbird eggs hatch in 10 days, usually before their victim's eggs. The young are larger and grow more rapidly, thus competing successfully against smaller nestlings.

Cowbirds are readily attracted with seed to bird feeders in May and June. A high-pitched, drawn out, rising "sqree-ee" is a distinctive part of their vocabulary.

Brown-headed Cowbird L 6½" (perched trio)
*   juvenile (top left) ♀   (center left) ♂ (upper right)*
Brewer's Blackbird L 8" ♀   and ♂ (on ground)

Z. M. Schultz

Yellow-headed Blackbird   ♀   ♂

Z. M. Schultz

L 8½"

YELLOW-HEADED BLACKBIRDS are the most conspicuous and distinctive birds of the great marshes east of the Cascades. They are not restricted to large marshes. A colony may be found on any suitable cattail or rush patch. Small numbers occur in summer northward through the Willamette Valley, but elsewhere west of the Cascades it is a rather rare migrant.

In many of its habits the Yellow-head is quite similar to the Red-winged Blackbird and they often join in feeding forays to nearby farmlands or feedlots. Yellow-headed Blackbirds are rarely observed in winter as most migrate southward.

The gaudy male can hardly be confused with any other bird. The female and young birds are the only blackbirds showing a yellow breast and face pattern.

The song of the male Yellow-headed Blackbird, heard continuously about the nesting marsh can hardly be described, but W. L. Dawson does it best as he writes: "Grasping a reed firmly in both fists, he leans foreward, and, after premonitory gulps and gasps, he succeeds in pressing out a wail of despairing agony which would do credit to a dying catamount." One of the most unusual of bird calls.

162

R. B. Horsfall

Western Meadowlark L 8½″

The **WESTERN MEADOWLARK,** Oregon's State Bird, stands apart from all other birds in this region. Its yellow breast, black bib and white outer tail feathers are distinctive. It is found in open grassland areas. Residential developments are filling former open areas of lowlands, so the Meadowlark is declining in numbers locally. Fortunately, this is not occurring east of the Cascades.

The glorious song of the Meadowlark, unlike many other birds, is sung from an open perch rather than from seclusion. Sometimes the song is sung in flight. A trill and loud call are also given. Meadowlarks are territorial during nesting season but in fall and winter join in small flocks. Most Meadowlarks migrate south for the winter and reappear in March.

Food consists largely of animal life, mostly insects, but some vegetation including seeds is also taken.

The **NORTHERN ORIOLE** is found along cottonwood-lined streams throughout the Northwest, but it is somewhat irregular west of the Cascades, especially in Western Washington and British Columbia. People inquire about this bird because of the male's brilliant orange, black and white plumage. Their pendulous nests suspended from limbs overhanging lowland rivers also arouse interest. These orioles come in pairs and are here only during the summer. Their noisy chatter breaks frequently into a distinctive piping song.

The western race of this bird is known as BULLOCK'S ORIOLE. It and the similar Baltimore Oriole of the eastern states are now considered to be the same species.

The **WESTERN TANAGER** male can't be confused with any other species because of its bright yellow body and red head. The female, however, often gives identification problems, but no other greenish yellow bird of its size occurs in similar habitat. Western Tanagers are common in summer in the coniferous forests throughout the Northwest, especially if some deciduous trees are intermixed. Large flocks are often observed in migration.

In summer we hear more than we see of the Western Tanager since it stays in the upper canopy of large conifers. It has a song very much like an American Robin or Black-headed Grosbeak. The call is "pid-a-dik" or "pa-dik."

Food of tanagers is about 80% insects; the rest is fruit and seeds.

Bullock's Oriole ♂
L 7" ♀

Western Tanager ♂
L 6¼" ♀

R. B. Horsfall

164

Black-headed Grosbeak L 7¼"
♂ *(above)* ♀ *(below)*

The **BLACK-HEADED GROSBEAK** male is another brilliantly colored bird which is easy to identify. It arrives from Mexico in May and immediately begins singing a glorified Robin-like song which can be mistaken only for a Robin or Western Tanager. The song is fuller, longer and richer than that of a Robin and sometimes ends with a trill. A loud squeak is given as a call.

This grosbeak does not occur here in flocks as does the Evening Grosbeak but comes as singles into urban areas having generous stands of trees and shrubs. Stream bottoms are also favored habitat along with open woods near water. Deciduous growth is favored.

This is one of our noisiest birds during the height of the singing season, but by mid-July is almost silent. The duller females are not seen as often as the males.

Food preferences are equally divided between animal life, mostly insects, and vegetable matter consisting of fruit and seeds. Because of the latter, it is possible to attract Black-headed Grosbeaks to a bird feeder. Because they are highly territorial, only one or two will come at a time.

The **EVENING GROSBEAK** comes in flocks which feed in one area for a few days and then move on, sometimes not to reappear for several years at a given site. When they occur, they bring numerous comments because of their contrasting plumage in yellow and black, and greenish-yellow, parrot-like bills.

In cities they feed on the ground as well as in trees, taking seeds and buds of willows, maple and elms. While feeding and in flight, they continually give their "pteer" whistle-like call. They also take wild fruits and some insects in summer. However, their heavy bill is adapted to cracking hard seeds and a flock can go through ten pounds of sunflower seeds at a feeder in a matter of a few hours.

These grosbeaks most often invade our cities and towns in early spring. During summer and winter, they tend to occur in the mountains where they extract seeds from cones of coniferous trees. Only during nesting season do the flocks split up.

♀ *Evening Grosbeak L 7¼"* ♂

R. B. Horsfall

♂
American Goldfinch L 4¼"
♂ *Lesser Goldfinch (below) L 3¾"*
♀

The **AMERICAN GOLDFINCH,** Washington's State Bird, was formerly referred to as Willow Goldfinch and is popularly called "Wild Canary." A small, bright yellow bird with black wings and a black crown patch that sings from a utility wire along a country road in spring has to be this species. In winter, however, the male's bright colors give way to somber hues like those of the female.

In summer goldfinches occur as singles, pairs, or small groups. In winter great flocks develop that whirl away and then make a quick return, often to the same spot. A mixture of trees, brush and fields, particularly where there is an abundance of weeds, provides ideal habitat. River bottoms are favored by wintering flocks.

Goldfinches sing like canaries and have a flight song or call which can be worded "perchickaree."

Greatest enemy of the goldfinch may be the weed killer 2-4,d since these birds like to feed on thistle, dandelion, and other seeds of the composite family. They nest late, after the seeds of these plants have matured.

The **LESSER GOLDFINCH,** formerly called Green-backed Goldfinch, is duller in color and slightly smaller than the American Goldfinch. The song is less musical and, overall, the bird is not as sociable, usually occurring here in summer as pairs. It is common only in localized areas, and barely gets into Washington. Open areas with a scattering of trees and brush are used and, to some extent, they come into city gardens. Water for drinking and bathing is important to them.

♀ *Cassin's Finch* ♂ *above*

L. M. McQueen

♂ *Purple Finch* ♀

The **PURPLE FINCH** is one of many medium sized finches in which the males carry considerable red color. Even intermediate bird students have difficulty separating this bird from the more common House Finch. The Purple Finch has a chunkier body and bill than the House Finch, and the male lacks striping on the flanks. Female Purple Finches often have a broad white line extending back from the eye—a feature lacking in the House Finch. Songs and calls, when learned, also help separate the two.

In summer Purple Finches occur in mixed forests, particularly along hillsides adjoining valleys. For the winter they tend to go to willows and cottonwoods along river bottoms. It appears they may have been partially replaced in urban areas by the House Finch.

The Purple Finch's song is a loud, clear warble given from March to July. Calls include a metallic "pic" and a slightly musical "ah-ree-ah." First year males which look like females also sing and nest.

The term "purple" apparently comes from the fact that the purple color of biblical times was a wine red. This in itself helps distinguish male Purple Finches from male House Finches which tend toward an orange red.

Purple Finches are primarily seed eaters but in spring take buds and some insects. Fruit is consumed in summer.

At high elevations and east of the Cascades, the Purple Finch is replaced by the similar **CASSIN'S FINCH,** which differs in having a bright red crown and rose colored breast and rump patch. The female Cassin's Finch is similar to the female Purple Finch but is much paler showing more contrast to its dark markings.

The **HOUSE FINCH** or California Linnet invaded Western Oregon and Washington in the early 1940s and is now one of our most common city and farm birds along with the House Sparrow. House Finches have adapted so well to man that they are extending their range farther north into Canada and eastward toward the Atlantic seaboard. Even concrete and asphalt-covered portions of cities are home for House Finches provided there is an occasional shrub or tree. A great variety of nest sites are used ranging from cavities to dense shrubs. Two broods are raised in some years.

House Finches are confused with Purple Finches, but they do not extend as far into forested areas as Purple Finches. For other differences between the two, see the Purple Finch description.

For food, House Finches like variety but prefer vegetable matter including seeds, buds and blossoms; some insects are taken. They can be a pest to fruit growers. Damage to blueberries occurs locally. At bird feeders they are prominent recipients of seeds, especially those of sunflowers.

House Finches will sing their rollicky warbling song with its numerous variations from early spring through the summer, but are comparatively silent in winter when they tend to flock together and occur more in the country, often in company with goldfinches and Pine Siskins. In flocks, they are roadside wire sitters.

There is great variation in the red coloring of the male, from pink to red to yellow.

House Finch L 5¼"   ♂   ♀

Z. M. Schultz

The **LAZULI BUNTING** resembles a goldfinch in habits and song, but the male with his turquoise head is unlike any other bird in this area. Buntings frequent brushy areas interspersed with trees and grassy openings. They arrive in late April and the males sing from conspicuous perches, such as utility wires, into June when they seem to fade away.

Lazuli Bunting   R. B. Horsfall
L 4½″ ♀ and ♂ (below)

The **PINE SISKIN,** a goldfinch-like bird with brown streaked and yellow-tinted plumage, is abundant in our area. Its blending plumage causes it to be overlooked. Siskins are highly social year-round and are great wanderers. They move through valleys and mountains alike depending on food availability.

Pine Siskins sometimes accompany goldfinches to feed on dandelion seeds. This affords an opportunity to learn the Pine Siskin's call, a thin, lispy or scratchy, upward slurring "swi-sieee." Once familiar with this and their other wheezy calls, including some given in flight, one recognizes their abundance. They are high fliers while traveling from treetop to treetop where they forage on seeds of conifers and alders. They often extract seeds while hanging upside down.

The **RED CROSSBILL** is a chunky, restless, nomadic finch of coniferous forests that possesses crossed mandibles adapted to extracting seeds from cones. Crossbill plumages exhibit wide color variations from olive grays through yellows to reds. Sharp "kip, kip, kip" notes identify a flock of these unpredictable wanderers. They have no regard for the seasons and may nest at any time.

170

Pine Siskin
L 4½″
(upper right)

Red Crossbill
L 5½″
♂ and ♀ (center)
R.B. Horsfall

White-winged Crossbill ♀   ♂

Z. M. Schultz
L 5¾″

The **WHITE-WINGED CROSSBILL** is similar to the common Red Crossbill but for its bright wing bars and soft canary-like song. They are uncommon and irregular winter visitors southward to Washington and Northeastern Oregon, occasionally visiting other Oregon localities. A few may even remain to nest in favored areas. Both crossbills my be seen in the same flock.

The Robin-like **PINE GROSBEAK** is similar to the crossbills but is much larger and has a large finch bill. It is an uncommon resident of the high mountain forests of the Cascades and eastward. They may appear in lowland areas anywhere in the Northwest during the winter months. These lowland records seem to correspond with cyclic invasions of northern migrants.

Pine Grosbeak   ♀   ♂   **L 7¾″**
Z. M. Schultz

Rufous-sided Towhee L 7¼″ ♂

R. B. Horsfall
Oregon Junco L 5¼″ ♂

DARK-EYED JUNCO is a name applied to a number of different juncos which form a complex involving many races and hybrids. Included in the complex is the OREGON JUNCO, which is most prominent locally.

Juncos are medium-sized, dainty featured finches. Oregon Junco males have black heads; the females are grayer.

Juncos are often called "snowbirds" since they linger in flocks throughout our countryside in winter and gather about bird feeders, especially when snow is present.

Locally, juncos nest from coast to mountains. They pair in early spring along the edges of timber where grass and brush are present. Edges of clearcuts are favored nesting areas, but they will nest in sparsely settled urban areas as well.

Winter flocks move in unison, showing white outer tail feathers which are a key identification feature.

Juncos are ground feeders and readily accept numerous kinds of seeds and suet at the bird feeder. In our forests they feed extensively on fallen conifer seeds.

Their song is a trill without any change in pitch from beginning to end. A lispy call note and a scolding note are also given—the latter near a nest and the former when a flock is flushed.

The **RUFOUS-SIDED TOWHEE** was formerly referred to as the Spotted Towhee, and our local subspecies has been called the Oregon Towhee. It is one of our most common backyard birds so long as there is a plentiful supply of shrubs or brush. Its black neck and head contrast sharply with reddish flanks and white belly, and it has fiery red eyes and white spots on the back.

This bird occurs in pairs or family groups, never in flocks, and is basically a ground bird around thick brush and dark places. It kicks leaves backwards to uncover insects, but it also takes seeds and does not hesitate to come to a bird feeder despite its shyness.

This towhee has an unmusical song given in early spring—a drawn out "tow-eee" that is repeated monotonously from a low shrub or tree.

The **BROWN TOWHEE** occurs along the edges of Southwestern Oregon valleys southward. Its habits are much like the previous species.

Brown Towhee L 7¼"

Z. M. Schultz

Green-tailed Towhee

A. C. Fisher
L 6¼"

The **GREEN-TAILED TOWHEE** looks and acts like a large secretive sparrow. Its unique greenish coloration can only be noted in very bright sunlight. The reddish crown and white throat is distinctive. It is a summer resident of the dry brushlands found to the east of the Cascade Crest but not in the sagebrush deserts. It ranges northward into Southeastern Washington, and only rarely in migration west of the Cascades.

The **SAGE SPARROW** is a summer resident of the vast sagebrush deserts and adjacent grasslands east of the Cascade Mountains, a few remain to winter. Its plain grayish-brown plumage and secretive ways render it quite inconspicuous although it is an abundant bird. If one is observed sitting on top of a sagebrush the white facial markings on its grayish head is distinctive. The similar **BLACK-THROATED SPARROW** (not illustrated) occurring northward into Southeastern Oregon has a deep black throat and more contrasting facial markings.

Brewer's Sparrow

Z. M. Schultz
L 4½"

The **BREWER'S SPARROW** is an abundant summer resident of the sagebrush deserts east of the Cascade Mountains. It is a plain plumaged cousin of the Chipping Sparrow with fine grayish-brown streaking on its head. The long canary-like song, heard coming from such a small bird, is quite surprising. Brewer's Sparrows occasionally visit other areas in migration but seldom occur west of the Cascades.

The similarly plumaged **CLAY-COLORED SPARROW** (not illustrated) occurs locally in eastern Washington and rarely in other sections of the Northwest. The broad whitish stripe down the center of the crown and more contrasting facial pattern is as distinctive as its buzzy call notes.

175

Sage Sparrow L 5"
Z. M. Schultz

R. B. Horsfall

Chipping Sparrow L 4¾"

Vesper Sparrow L 5½"   Savannah Sparrow L 4¾"

The **CHIPPING SPARROW** is a rather distinctive small sparrow with brick red cap, white eye stripe, and gray breast. It occurs in open woodlands and borders between fields and woods during summer and, to a limited extent, comes into the lawns of small towns.

Its song is an insect-like trill which can be distinguished from the junco in that the notes are much closer together. They usually occur here as singles or pairs.

The **SAVANNAH SPARROW** frequents pastures and other open grasslands, mostly in summer. It is seldom seen in winter. One would hardly notice this bird except for its weak insect-like song given from a fence wire or post. A yellow stripe is present over the eye of some races, but otherwise this is a small, light brown streaked sparrow found in the country but not in the city. Like other small sparrows, its food is equally divided between seeds and insects, depending upon the season.

The **VESPER SPARROW**, slightly larger than a Savannah Sparrow, is another streaked brown sparrow which utilizes fence rows bordering grasslands, croplands and pastures. It has a clear, pleasing song. In flight, it shows conspicuous white outer tail feathers. It occurs here in summer only.

WHITE-CROWNED SPARROWS and **GOLDEN-CROWNED SPAR-ROWS** are relatively large "crowned" sparrows that often occur together during migration and in winter. The adult "White-crown" is identified by white stripes bordered by black on the crown, and immatures have red rather than white crown stripes. The Golden-crown Sparrow has a single yellow crown patch bordered by black. Immatures have only a faint patch of the yellow color.

Unlike the "Golden-crown," the "White-crown" occurs in summer as a common nesting species. A wide variety of habitats is utilized as nesting territories, but about our lowlands it prefers small farm fields interspersed with second growth timber. However, it accepts any open area, incuding the landscaped edges of the Stadium Freeway in downtown Portland.

Our local nesting subspecies was formerly called Puget Sound sparrow. It is a strong singer and commonly sings at night. It's call is a metallic "pink."

In winter White-crowned Sparrows from outside this area move in as small flocks to frequent fence rows and roadsides with Golden-crowned Sparrows. The flocks feed along edges of blackberry patches and other brush. When frightened they fly into the brush but soon reappear.

Golden-crowned Sparrows come from Canada and Alaska in September and remain until early May. Their melancholy "oh-dear-me" song which descends in pitch reaches a peak as they depart for the north in early May.

"Golden-crowns," along with "White-crowns," will frequent bird feeders to take seeds. Besides grass seedlings and weed seeds, they are also fond of buds, flowers, and vegetable seedlings.

Golden-crowned Sparrow, adult   White-crowned Sparrow, adult
L 6¼"   L 5¾"

R. B. Horsfall

Lark Sparrow   L 5¾"

The **LARK SPARROW** is a large crowned sparrow of the drier open meadows and farm lands east of the Cascade Mountains and Southwest Oregon. It occasionally visits other Northwest areas. Large flocks occur in migration, otherwise they are widely scattered. The chestnut colored head pattern and central breast spot are distinctive.

LINCOLN'S SPARROWS are Song Sparrow-like birds of mountain bogs and wet meadows. They occur throughut the Northwest in migration and small numbers winter west of the Cascades. The Lincoln's Sparrow resembles a pale Song Sparrow but has a distinctive buffy wash across the streaked breast. It is obviously shyer than other sparrows and seldom strays from heavy cover.

Lincoln's Sparrow   L 4¾"

Song Sparrow L 5½"   Fox Sparrow L 6¼"

The **SONG SPARROW** is one of our most widely distributed birds. Each major brush patch has one or more pairs, and they are found throughout the country and city. Our nesting Song Sparrows remain in the same vicinity throughout the year, but they are joined during fall, winter and spring by migratory Song Sparrows from other areas.

Song Sparrows are beautiful songsters with a large repertoire given in all but the dry days of late summer. When disturbed, they have a metallic scolding note.

Song Sparrows feed on the ground, taking both insects and seeds. They are common about bird feeders but rarely come in flocks because most of the year they are highly territorial and defend their areas against other Song Sparrows.

In recent years the Song Sparrows of our area have become heavily parasitized by Cowbirds—a new immigrant to this area. It is not uncommon to see a Song Sparrow feeding a Cowbird which is larger than the sparrow.

The **FOX SPARROW** is a large, brown sparrow resembling a Song Sparrow but showing blotchier spotting on the breast. It occurs in the brush of our valleys in winter, often as singles or with Song Sparrows and other sparrows. Several races come into our area from northern latitudes to winter. In summer, Fox Sparrows do not occur in the lowlands.

Fox Sparrows are shyer than Song Sparrows and tend to stick to heavy cover and shadows. They kick leaves backwards, using both feet simultaneously, much like a towhee, and feed on the ground, taking insects and seeds. Occasionally they will come to bird feeders for seeds.

Except for a scolding note, they are quiet, but may sing before departing for nesting areas in late April or early May.

INDEX

INDEX

INDEX

INDEX

INDEX